The American Colonial Experience

An Essay in National Origins

The American Colonial Experience
An Essay in National Origins

PAUL GOODMAN
University of California, Davis

FRANK OTTO GATELL
University of California, Los Angeles

HOLT, RINEHART AND WINSTON, INC.
New York   Chicago   San Francisco   Atlanta
Dallas   Montreal   Toronto   London   Sydney

Preface

This book is designed to provide students with a brief, analytical introduction to the history of America's colonial period. We have treated only a limited number of events, leaving out many that conventionally are included in surveys of this period. We have chosen, rather, to probe more deeply the major historical developments of this period. We have also shifted the balance somewhat in favor of analysis and away from narrative in the hope that students will grasp more clearly *why* the American colonies developed as they did. For students who wish to probe more deeply into one of the major themes treated in Chapters TWO TO FIVE, we have reprinted, following those chapters, substantial selections from four original sources—William Bradford's history of the Pilgrims, Thomas Phillips' account of the slave trade, Andrew Hamilton's defense of freedom of the press, and Reverend Andrew Burnaby's account of travel at the end of the colonial period.

P. G.
F. O. G.

Davis, California
Los Angeles, California
December 1969

Contents

Preface *v*

INTRODUCTION
The Relevance of the American Past *1*

CHAPTER ONE
The Expansion of Europe *6*

CHAPTER TWO
Plantations in the Wilderness *20*
Document: The Pilgrim Experience
William Bradford *42*

CHAPTER THREE
Roots of Expansion *68*
Document: The African Slave Trade
The Voyage of the Hannibal *89*

CHAPTER FOUR
From Plantations to Commonwealths *103*
Document: Colonial Politics and Freedom of the Press
Andrew Hamilton *124*

CHAPTER FIVE
Sources of American Nationality *141*
Document: A British Visitor to the Colonies, 1759–1760
Reverend Andrew Burnaby *160*

CHAPTER SIX
The Colonial Legacy *175*

INDEX *181*

Introduction

The Relevance of the American Past

Americans live in the youngest of the world's great nations. They derive their identity from different sources than Russians, Chinese, Britons, or Germans. The citizens of these nations trace their ancestry back hundreds of years to those who lived in the same place as their descendants, who spoke a distinctive language similar to their descendants' tongue, and who created a culture that persisted through centuries, enriched and made more complex by each succeeding generation. Americans, however, have inhabited their land for only a few hundred years; they speak a language borrowed from the Old World; and their culture is both young and derived from the mingling of many foreign ingredients.

Peopled by men of many faiths from many nations, America derives its identity from a commitment to belief in the dignity of man, the right of every person to life, liberty, and the pursuit of happiness. Attracted by the promise of American life, millions crossed the oceans to become Americans by adoption, not birth. For most of their history Americans—that is white Americans—have been confident of their own capacity to determine their fate and to make of themselves what they will. Only recently have black Americans come to articulate such hopes.

1

Whites have thought of this country as a model republic whose example inspired the downtrodden to migrate to the New World in search of a better life. Most Americans still think it remains man's best hope: a land of opportunity, with great natural wealth but without aristocratic, privileged groups monopolizing life's best rewards; the home of those who left the past behind them, hoping to start afresh in a New World, a world free from material impoverishment because hard work and unusual talents were usually rewarded; free also from tyranny over the mind and spirit, because neither church nor state dictated what men could think and imagine.

No nation's sense of identity reflects reality literally. Americans have not always been optimistic. They have not always solved their problems peacefully; opportunities have not always been available to all according to merit; and diligence and talent have often gone unrewarded. Men have sometimes been afraid to expose their inner beliefs to the scorn and reprisals of bigoted majorities or repressive minorities. Yet their self-image is rooted in reality: Americans have enjoyed an unusual degree of material abundance and substantial opportunity to share in that abundance; they have had more to say about running their society than most people elsewhere; and they have been freer to observe peculiar customs, hold unorthodox beliefs, and worship different Gods.

Today, some Americans radically dissent from the values and institutions most accept. They argue that Americans have sacrificed man's inner needs for love, cooperation, and communal peace on the altar of a materialist outlook which has made citizens competitive and aggressive, taught them to worship power and wealth, and to regard persons as commodities rather than as human beings capable of realizing their full potential. Critics argue that a society whose highest loyalty is to technology and the marketplace, and the creature comforts these make possible, dooms men to alienation, robs them of inner peace and leaves them seeking refuge in the pain-killer of escapist entertainment and forced togetherness. Ultimately it may lead men to destroy life itself.

Neither the critics who see only darkness in America, nor the contented who see only light possess the truth. Dissenters must acknowledge that their society has produced would-be saviors, free to dissent radically from established values and modes of life, and free to seek change. And those who reject the radical critique must acknowledge, however, that all is not well in a republic which produces sizable minorities of gifted and sensitive persons who reject the American way of life. To understand more clearly this American crisis, to evaluate intelligently the roots of today's uneasiness, one must look into the past to discover the sources of American culture.

Sometime before the American colonies became the United States, perceptive Europeans noted that "a new race of men" inhabited England's North American provinces. By the time these colonies won independence, a widespread sense already existed among the citizens that they differed from the English, Irish, Scotch, Dutch, Germans, and other nationalities they had left behind in their home lands. This transformation of the European into the American occurred during America's colonial period, the 175 years after the first settlement early in the seventeenth century until the declaration of nationhood in 1776. Those formative years laid the foundations for a powerful nation.

The distinctive characteristics of colonial America later became common characteristics of modern society. Here in the New World material abundance and the diffusion of wealth enabled the majority of white citizens to live in relative comfort and to aspire to improve their condition. Government in the colonies was far more sensitive to the wishes and interests of the people at large than in Europe at that time. Here a sizable percentage of adult males could vote, and though people generally deferred to the wisdom, judgment, and leadership of the "better" sort—the colonial elite—the terms of political participation were broadening and pointing in the direction of popular government, at a time when kings and aristocrats monopolized power elsewhere. America also was the birthplace of religious freedom. By the end of the colonial period, not only were men free to worship as they wished, but the ties between church and state had weakened, pointing to the separation of the sacred from the secular during the revolutionary era. Finally, birth counted for less and individual achievement for more in determining a family's status than was the case in Europe. Here there were no hereditary, privileged classes but a relatively fluid social structure with extensive opportunities for upward mobility.

America, wrote the French visitor to the colonies, Hector St. John de Crèvecoeur in *Letters from an American Farmer,* displays "one diffusive scene of happiness reaching from the sea-shores to the last settlements on the borders of the wilderness." The most striking difference between the Old World and the New was that most colonists were freeholders. The ownership of property gave men pride and independence as well as the right to vote. In the words of Crèvecoeur's American farmer: "The instant I enter on my own land, the bright idea of property, of exclusive right, of independence exalts my mind . . . on it is founded our rank, our freedom, our power as citizens, our importance as inhabitants."

Out of their experiences as colonists, Americans formulated the revolutionary principles on which to found a new nation. Their belief in individual liberty, the equality of man, and freedom of thought distinguished the Americans from other nations. In the eighteenth century it provided the basis of their identity as a people. In our own time as in the past, the gap between the republic's professed ideals and such realities of American society as racial injustice and poverty amid plenty creates a dynamic tension. The way Americans have resolved the conflict between their beliefs and their behavior has shaped their history and will determine their future.

Suggestions for Further Reading

Suggestions for further reading following each chapter are highly selective. Works available in paperback are starred (*). Students should consult Clarence Ver Steeg, *The Formative*

Years: 1607–1763 (1964) and Curtis P. Nettels, *Roots of American Civilization* (1938) for additional references.

General Works on the American Colonial Period

Clarence Ver Steeg, *The Formative Years* (1964); Curtis P. Nettels, *Roots of American Civilization* (1938); Daniel Boorstin, *The Americans: The Colonial Experience* (1958)*; Paul Goodman, ed., *Essays in American Colonial History* (1967)*; W. F. Craven, *The Colonies in Transition 1660–1713* (1968).*

Contemporary Accounts

J. Hector St. John de Crèvecoeur, *Letters from an American Farmer* (1782)*; Gottlieb Mittelberger, *Journey to Pennsylvania,* O. Handlin and John Clive, eds. (1960); Peter Kalm, *A Journey to North America* (1770); Andrew Hamilton, *Gentleman's Progress,* Carl Bridenbaugh, ed. (1948); William Bradford, *Of Plymouth Plantations,* S. E. Morison, ed. (1952); Andrew Burnaby, *Travels through North America* (1775)*; Charles Woodmason, *The Carolina Backcountry,* R. J. Hooker, ed., (1953); Hugh Jones, *The Present State of Virginia,* R. L. Morton, ed. (1956)*.

Chapter One

The Expansion of Europe

For thousands of years the Western Hemisphere lay hidden from the great civilizations of East and West. But toward the end of the fifteenth century Europe discovered a New World. During the next hundred years the Spanish, Portuguese, French, English, and Dutch spilled blood and gained treasure exploring this new continent and staking out imperial claims. Almost overnight Western Europeans broadened their horizons. For centuries following the collapse of Rome, European civilization had contracted, hemmed in by newly risen and hostile forces, first the Arabs, mobilized by the faith of Islam, later by the Ottoman Turks, and always by the impenetrable barrier the ocean placed in the way of Europe's westward thrust.

All that changed during the century after Columbus discovered America. Christians repelled the Turkish threat at the gates of Vienna in 1529, and Europeans gained a foothold in North Africa from which Islam had launched its invasion of Christendom. The rough waters of the Atlantic now carried European vessels to the far reaches of the globe. It was no accident that ships bearing the flags of Spain, Portugal, and other European kingdoms, and not those of China, Japan, or other Eastern nations found a new world; nor was the timing of America's discovery accidental. The Western Hemisphere became Europe's prize because what had been happening in the Old World long before Columbus set sail in August, 1492, prepared Europeans for the role of successful colonizers and empire builders.

The Preconditions of Expansion

In the vanguard of European expansion stood Portugal and Spain. The Iberian peninsula had played a minor role in European affairs until the Age of Columbus when its soldiers and sailors carved out great empires. The Spaniards and Portuguese were first in the race for empire because they possessed the necessary resources and expansionist attitudes which other colonizing kingdoms did not acquire until later.

Overseas expansion was the work of strong, unified states. Internal unity gave Spain and Portugal a head start, just as, on the other hand, Germany and Italy lagged behind in the scramble for foreign possessions until their own unification toward the end of the nineteenth century. During the Middle Ages many great and lesser nobles shared political power and the king was rarely master of his kingdom. In the modern state which began to emerge in the fifteenth century, the king increasingly centralized power in his own hands. Spain, as did other parts of Europe, comprised some large and many small feudal principalities recognizing no supreme secular power.

Necessity, however, compelled Spaniards to unite behind a strong king before other countries saw the need. For seven centuries all or part of Spain lay under Arab rule. Christian reconquest proved slow and difficult. It ended the same year Columbus sailed west under the patronage of the dynasty that succeeded in expelling the Moors. This was the work of Isabella of Castile and Ferdinand of Aragon who joined forces against the Moors and subdued their Spanish rivals in the name of Christian unity and national liberation. Until England and France overcame their internal disunity, they were not ready to compete.

Portugal took the lead in organizing public and private resources for expansion. This small kingdom, unified even earlier than Spain, and inspired by a Catholic faith nourished in centuries of struggle with the Moslems, conquered the city of Ceuta in North Africa (1415) and planned further assaults against Arab power. The weakening or destruction of Moslem control of the Mediterranean also offered rich material rewards to Europe's merchants and trading companies once they gained more direct access to the oriental spices which were then staples in international trade. The strategic shortcut, the Portuguese believed, lay not in assaulting Islam directly in the Mediterranean but in sailing down the west coast of Africa to attack the enemy from the rear.

During the fifteenth century, the Portuguese colonized the Azores and Canary Islands far out in the Atlantic, trafficked in gold and slaves, and explored the African coastline. In 1488 Bartholomew Dias reached the Cape of Good Hope at Africa's southernmost tip and ten years later, Vasco da Gama completed a voyage around Africa to India and back. These and other expeditions, not all of them successful, cost money. But by mobilizing a small portion of the national wealth for exploration the Portuguese crown eventually profited enormously.

The crown did more than finance exploration; it attempted to solve technical problems that impeded long ocean voyages into strange and dangerous seas. During the later Middle Ages, navigational advances had been made but ships were still designed for short, relatively safe voyages, and scientific aids were often inadequate for the ambitious, dangerous undertakings Portugal contemplated. Prince Henry the Navigator (1394–1460), son of John I, established an institute where scholars and experienced seamen pooled their knowledge and applied it to solving practical problems. By the sixteenth century European vessels were the best in the world. Capitalizing on cumulative scientific advances in shipbuilding and navigation, the Portuguese built superior and better armed vessels. With cannons mounted on their vessels, Portuguese captains enjoyed an overwhelming advantage over slower, clumsier, and undergunned enemy fleets. Portugal thereby undermined Arab control of the spice trade and gained command of the Indian Ocean, establishing naval bases and fortresses at the sources of supply in India, China, and the East Indies. Its success foreshadowed the next four centuries during which Europe's scientific and technological advantages made it the dominant continent.

For Spain, as for Portugal, exploration and expansion were outlets for the energy and enthusiasm created by success in the reconquest campaign against Islam. The methods of reconquest at home—mobilizing power against the enemy, securing strong points, staking out claims, and acquiring dominion over defeated populations—all could be used to carry the flag abroad as well. Spain's seven hundred year crusading tradition led it to press into North Africa, but Spaniards also dreamed of finding newer areas to provide lands and booty to seize and "infidels" to convert.

Christopher Columbus (1451–1506), the son of a Genoese wool weaver, was an experienced seaman who believed that he could reach the East Indies by sailing west. Neither Portugal nor Spain, whose patronage he repeatedly sought, were willing to back him. The western seas were uncharted and Columbus thought the voyage practical only because he grossly underestimated the distance. His persistence finally paid off. After the fall of Granada, the last Moorish fortress, the Spanish crown, flushed with victory, appointed him Admiral of the Ocean Sea, viceroy and governor of whatever land he might discover. Jealous of Portuguese success, the Spaniards hoped to compete by finding a new route to the Orient via oceans yet unknown to their rivals.

With a fleet of three ships and a crew of ninety, Columbus, a superb sailor, sailed west. Nine weeks later, he sighted land in the Bahamas and soon discovered Cuba and Santo Domingo. In the next ten years he made three more voyages to America, believing each time that further exploration would bring him to the Indies. He died insisting that the large land mass he had found was an island, never realizing that he had discovered a fourth continent. Yet within his own lifetime this truth was gaining recognition, although for the next century explorers of many nations persisted in the quest for a passage to India through the Western Hemisphere.

The discovery of a new world shattered the medieval Christian belief in a static and finite universe with a fixed habitable portion of land, an island surrounded by hostile seas. Believing in the Fall of Man, the Christian perceived the world as a prison in which he must suffer and labor, destined by God to "take possession of the earth so far as he is able to do so by his own efforts" and to transform "it to meet his own needs." Columbus was driven by a mystical vision that he could conquer the unknown. After his voyage the universe no longer appeared so fixed or finite. For some it was now no longer a prison but instead a constant challenge to human courage, intelligence, and imagination.

European expansion rested on many interrelated foundations. Christian belief in the imperfection of the present sent restless men into the world to search for El Dorado and spread the faith. The powerful new nation-states provided political and administrative structures which harnessed scientific and technical knowledge, surplus capital, and the desire for material gain in the cause of exploration and empire. As nations pushed through the geographical limits that had once confined medieval Europe, they were entering a new era in the history of the West. The birth of modern science was unlocking the secrets of the universe. The centralized modern states were rationalizing government. And economic development was creating new wealth and possibilities for material achievement. The expansion of Europe was thus an expression of the dynamic forces transforming the West from a medieval to a modern civilization.

Varieties of Colonization: The Spanish Example

Each European nation entering the race for empire had a unique colonization experience. A nation's internal development prior to expansion, as well as opportunities and obstacles encountered in the New World, influenced the timing, direction, and methods of settlement. Latin America in the middle of the twentieth century still awaits modernizing revolutions that will transform outdated and unpopular social orders, which are in part legacies from colonial experience under Spain. Canada, first settled by the French, but acquired by England through military victory over France in 1763, still struggles to harmonize two antagonistic ethnic traditions, English and French, and to develop vast resources not yet exploited. Like the former Spanish colonies, Canada had its national development shaped in part by its colonial history. Similarly the United States' experience as English colonies helped produce a nation decidely different from its neighbors to the north and south.

The Spanish empire was a vast estate whose economic, political, and religious life lay under royal control. Though the crown employed private adventurers to finance initial conquest and settlement, it carefully prevented them from acquiring too much power. Superior organization and military technology, coupled with strong faith in their cause, enabled a handful of Spaniards to gain mastery over several Indian civilizations. Hernando Cortes, with only 600 soldiers and sixteen horses, quickly subdued the Aztecs in Mexico. Francisco Pizarro, with 180 soldiers and thirty-seven horses, conquered the Incas in Peru. Once the Spaniards broke the power of the most advanced Indian cultures, they were free to construct a new social order.

Faithful soldiers received grants of land and the command of Indian labor, while the merchants of Seville enjoyed a monopoly of the transatlantic trade. The Church undertook vast campaigns to convert the Indians, thus helping to make them more resigned to Spanish rule, and in the process acquired valuable grants of land and taxing powers. The crown, however, controlled the church, its revenues, and appointments. It also carefully limited the rights of large planters, denying them representative institutions in order to stifle the rise of a powerful aristocracy. Madrid, the center of all political authority, made decisions, leaving little initiative to local functionaries who could not lay out a new town or even decide on the width of a street without orders from home.

Farming took place on large estates controlled by the crown, the Church, and Spaniards who migrated to form the local elite. During three centuries of Spanish rule, only 300,000 Europeans came to America; a great many of them were fortune seekers, minor nobility, and gentry who regarded manual labor as degrading. Since the crown desired to keep its colonies free of alien racial and religious elements, it barred Jews, Moors, and any except Spanish Catholics. It also excluded Spanish commercial interests other than the Sevillian monopoly. The Spanish peasantry had not yet undergone an agricultural revolution which elsewhere forced farmers off the land and created a large reservoir of potential immigrants. Lacking a displaced peasantry or numerous religious dissenters, since the Protestant Reformation did not make much headway in the Iberian peninsula, the Spaniards relied on Indian and later on African labor, either as slaves or as peons tied to the land by debt and obligations which guaranteed planters a stable work force.

Spain extracted great wealth from America. For a century, New World mines yielded gold and silver in abundance. And plantations produced tropical staples such as tobacco and sugar. But mining and agricultural technologies were primitive and there were few incentives to improve them. A wealthy colonial elite preferred to live comfortably, or return to Spain, rather than reinvest capital and exercise initiative to increase productivity. An American merchant class did not flourish because Seville monopolized imports and exports, and the principal market for imports was a small luxury-consuming elite. Most of the population remained impoverished. Economic growth consequently lagged.

The Spaniards erected impressive public buildings and founded universities which had no equals in size or importance in the English colonies, but their principal legacy was an exploitative social system that enriched crown, Church, and a small European elite at the expense of Indians and Negroes held in peonage or slavery. Much of the wealth of Latin America is still concentrated in a few hands, and the great mass of impoverished peasants have little stake in the existing social order. The ruling elements seem unwilling or incapable of modernizing and reforming their societies before revolutionary forces sweep them away as happened in Communist Cuba. Today's concentration of wealth in the hands of a few repeats the colonial past. The average standard of living is low and there are few strong representative governments, a condition which hinders the development of stable, democratic societies in Latin America.

Spaniards established their American empire a century before England planted its first permanent settlements in the New World, but their example did not become England's model. The English methods of colonization, though influenced in the beginning by Spanish experience, differed because English society on the eve of colonization bore little resemblance to imperial Spain.

The Expansion of England

England's internal condition long delayed its entrance into the competition for empire. While Spain came under control of a powerful dynasty in the fifteenth century, England was torn apart by civil war among rival claimants of the throne—The Wars of the Roses. Finally, in 1485, a new dynasty under the leadership of Henry Tudor methodically restored order, subdued resisting noblemen, and made the monarchy master of England.

The Tudors accumulated power by undermining the authority of potential rivals and by building a broad base of support among newer elements whose prosperity depended, in part, on royal favor. The crown forced great nobles to disband their private armies. A reformed system of royal justice penetrated the countryside and the king forced his will upon the local notables. The financial weakness of other monarchs had severely restricted their freedom of action by making them dependent on others. The Tudors avoided expensive wars and otherwise managed their revenues carefully, lessening dependence on the nobles or Parliament. By the time of Henry VIII (1509–1547), the Tudors had stabilized their rule. Eager to perpetuate the dynasty, Henry VIII sought a male heir whose succession, he thought, was less likely to stir opposition than a female's. The king hoped that a new wife would produce a male heir but the pope refused to grant him a divorce. He then joined Martin Luther and other Protestants in rejecting Rome as the authentic voice of Christianity.

The English Reformation gave the crown control over the resources and influence of the dispossessed Roman Church. Many Englishmen whose spiritual needs no longer found adequate expression in Catholic worship and who resented Rome's influence applauded the change. By confiscating the monasteries and granting their lands to supporters, the Tudors encouraged the rise of wealthy new families whose interests became identified with those of the royal dynasty. The crown shrewdly worked through Parliament and these rising elements could usually be counted on to support the crown there, further strengthening its resources and influence. By strengthening Parliament, the monarchy gave its subjects the privilege of participating in decision-making, a privilege that was, in the next century, ultimately expanded at the expense of royal authority.

At the same time that England experienced political modernization which consolidated power in the hands of the monarchy and broadened the terms of participation, its economic system likewise underwent change. England became more productive but also more unstable as economic development brought major dislocations.

Most Englishmen lived on the land and labored to satisfy their own wants. But now production for markets at home and abroad became increasingly important, as did commercial and industrial enterprise. In the sixteenth century, population swelled from three to four million inhabitants and the city of London more than doubled in size reaching a population of 200,000 by 1600. This growth depended in part on a surge in national wealth which came from more efficient methods of agriculture and the development of new sources of wealth in industry and commerce. The more enterprising landowners, large and small, found it profitable to acquire and consolidate the lands of poorer grain farmers. On the enclosed, larger holdings they raised sheep and marketed their wool abroad where it was manufactured into cloth. The enclosure movement, which had begun in the late Middle Ages, increased in tempo in the sixteenth century, pushing farmers off their lands without providing them alternative employment. As a result, "sturdy beggars" roamed the English countryside, often drifting into London in search of jobs. They gave vivid and tragic proof that English agriculture was more and more a way of making money rather than a way of life. Unemployment led some to believe that England was overpopulated and could profitably employ surplus labor in overseas colonies.

The export first of raw wool and then cloth to the continent of Europe had long been the principal item in English commerce. England led all Europe in cloth production and during the first half of the sixteenth century exports boomed, stimulating both wool production and cloth manufactures. As the English economy became more commercialized, regions began to specialize economically. Consequently, domestic markets for food, fuel, and clothing broadened in urban centers involved in overseas trade, and villages and rural communities concentrated on the production of exports. At the same time new industries developed. Armaments made England self-sufficient in the implements of war and coal mining provided fuel in place of depleted woodlands for the growing towns.

Although growth in foreign trade and industrial enterprise produced greater national prosperity, they also sensitized the economy to frequent unpredictable changes in the marketplace. High prices encouraged farmers and merchants to expand production. Eventually supply exceeded demand and forced prices down. Currency manipulation by the crown to increase revenue altered the terms of trade, sometimes, but not always, to England's advantage. Political turmoil abroad and the growth of foreign competition wiped out traditional markets. Unfavorable weather meant poor harvests which reduced the income of farmers and, consequently, their purchasing power, hurting merchants, manufacturers, and those they employed. Recurrent changes in the level of business activity disrupted the productive system, though hopes for striking it rich in a boom year encouraged risk taking and entrepreneurial activity.

The crown attempted to cushion the impact of these changes which left some permanently, others temporarily, unemployed, and which endangered the public order by creating unrest and riots among the needy. The state provided relief for the destitute, restricted labor mobility, and attempted to slow down the progress of enclosure but it did not halt economic change. Nor did the Tudors wish to. As national income grew, their wealth and power grew accordingly, especially their power to defend England against foreign enemies.

Depression in the wool trade encouraged British merchants to diversify their activities and seek new outlets for investment capital. British merchants squeezed out foreign merchants who had once controlled Britain's overseas trade. The English began to import goods from faraway places for reexport to the Continent. Hoping to avoid antagonizing Spain, England did not initially compete with her rival in the New World. Henry VII gave only halfhearted support to John and Sebastian Cabot who explored the North American coast for England in 1497 and 1498 and his successors were too preoccupied with maintaining internal order and with defending England against foreign attacks to undertake colonial expansion. By the middle of the sixteenth century, however, the crown chartered companies to discover new trade routes without conflicting with Spanish colonial claims. The Cathay Company (1552) sought a northeast passage to the Indies through the Arctic Ocean. Its failure led another group of adventurers to charter the Muscovy Company (1553) which opened trade with Russia. At the same time the Eastland Company traded in the Baltic countries and the Levant Company (1580) penetrated the Mediterranean, finding new markets for British cloth and metals in Italy, Turkey, and along the Barbary coast of North Africa.

The trading company, a medieval institution, gained increasing importance and became more complex in the sixteenth century. Those organized as joint-stock companies sold shares, enabling them to raise substantial amounts of capital. New and risky enterprises in distant places which required convoys, forts, and warehouses were too dangerous to attract investors without political support, so the crown granted monopoly charters to these companies. The growing number of joint-stock companies testified to the vitality of commercial enterprise, the availability of investment capital, and the shrewd patronage of the state. The greatest prize, however, remained beyond England's reach as long as Spain barred the way to India and America. England's more advanced economy, however, enabled it to develop the productive potential of colonies far more successfully than did Spain, once Britain acquired overseas settlements.

Like her predecessors, Queen Elizabeth (1558–1603) had to guard against internal disorder and sought therefore to avoid, or at least to delay, war with Spain. The wealth gathered from America made Catholic Spain the most powerful nation in six-teenth-century Europe and a formidable enemy for Protestant England. Instead of reinvesting their new-found wealth in the colonies or in Spain itself, the Spaniards used it to finance grandiose wars of conquest in Europe. Officially England re-mained at peace until 1586, but Elizabeth permitted attacks on Spanish shipping by Sir Francis Drake and Sir Walter Raleigh while developing warships that were tougher and more ma-neuverable than Spain's. In 1588, the English defeated Spain's mighty invasion armada off the southeast coast of England, ending Spanish maritime supremacy and clearing the seas for Britain's thrust across the Atlantic.

By the beginning of the seventeenth century, England was ready for empire in Asia and America. A strong and ambitious monarchy ruled over a unified and prosperous kingdom, flushed with the victory over Spain. At the same time, economic devel-opment created new resources, incentives, and institutions for carrying the flag across the ocean. Self-confident and expansive, Englishmen looked forward to conquering new worlds far from home. In the same year in which the King James Bible appeared, the English court attended a performance of William Shakespeare's new play, *The Tempest*. Expressing the spirit of the age, the drama was set in a distant, unknown and remarkable land—

> O, wonder!
> How many goodly creatures are there here!
> How beauteous mankind is! O brave new world,
> That has such people in't!

Suggestions for Further Reading

European Background

Myron P. Gilmore, *The World of Humanism* (1952)*; J. H. Parry, *The Establishment of the European Hegemony* (1961)*; J. H. Parry, *The Age of Reconnaissance* (1963); Howard M. Jones, *O Strange New World* (1964)*.

Spain

J. H. Elliott, *Imperial Spain 1469–1716* (1963)*; Clarence H. Haring, *Spanish Empire in America* (1952)*; J. H. Parry, *The Spanish Seaborne Empire* (1966); Silvio Zavala, *New Viewpoints on the Spanish Colonization of America* (1943); Charles Gibson, *Spain in America* (1966)*; S. E. Morison, *Admiral of the Ocean Sea*, 2 vols. (1942); S. E. Morison, *Christopher Columbus, Mariner* (1955)*.

France

Sigmund Diamond, "An Experiment in 'Feudalism': French Canada in the Seventeenth Century," *William and Mary Quarterly*, 3rd series, vol. 18 (1961), pp. 1–34.

England

Geoffrey R. Elton, *England under the Tudors* (1956); A. L. Rowse, *The England of Elizabeth* (1950)*; *The Expansion of Elizabethan England* (1955)*; Howard M. Jones, *O Strange New World* (1964)*; Wallace Notestein, *The English People on the Eve of Colonization* (1954)*; *Crisis in Europe, 1560–1660,*

Trevor Aston, ed. (1965)*; E. Lipson, *Economic History of England*, vol. 2 (1931); Lawrence Stone, "State Control in Sixteenth-Century England," *Economic History Review*, vol. 17 (1947), pp. 103–120; F. J. Fisher, "Commercial Trends and Policy in Sixteenth-Century England," *Economic History Review*, vol. 10 (1946), pp. 95–117; R. H. Tawney, *The Agrarian Problem in the Sixteenth Century* (1912)*; Barry E. Supple, *Commercial Crisis and Change in England, 1600–1642* (1959); Richard H. Tawney, *Religion and the Rise of Capitalism* (1926)*; Michael Walzer, *The Revolution of the Saints* (1965)*; Carl Bridenbaugh, *Vexed and Troubled Englishmen, 1590–1642* (1968).

Chapter Two

Plantations in the Wilderness

Early in the seventeenth century thousands of Englishmen emigrated to North America, the start of a European exodus that lasted 300 years. By the end of the seventeenth century a quarter million people inhabited twelve colonial settlements between French Canada and Spanish Florida. The methods of settlement varied, because England, unlike Spain and France, adopted no systematic, uniform centrally administered plan for expansion. The crown played a limited role at first. Heavy reliance on private initiative and enterprise produced a distinctive pattern of origin and settlement for each colony. From the beginning, diversity and a capacity to adapt to unexpected and challenging circumstances colored the development of American society.

Despite the diverse origins of these first settlements, they shared assumptions about how to proceed, assumptions based on common traditions and familiar experiences. People who ventured abroad in search of gain or a better life did not anticipate the social disorganization they encountered. They expected to transfer intact to the New World, as Spaniards and Frenchmen did, patterns of social organization similar to those they left behind. Few imagined that they would create a radically new society. Yet the English, much more than their rivals, modified early colonization plans, at first in order to survive and later to prosper. Dependence upon voluntary, rather than state-controlled enterprise, facilitated this willingness to adjust. Political instability in England during the first colonizing century, and social disorganization within Britain also contributed. The crown was relatively inattentive to colonial affairs, and civil war (1641–1660) at home turned many Englishmen toward the attraction of new opportunities in North America.

Virginia

Twenty years after Sir Walter Raleigh discovered Virginia, the English established their first permanent colony in North America. Initial attempts to settle on Roanoke Island had failed because of insufficient resources. However, the three ships dispatched by the Virginia Company which sailed into Chesapeake Bay and founded Jamestown on May 24, 1607, came better prepared.

The Virginia Company, chartered by the crown in 1606, was the first of eleven major companies which invested heavily in the settlement of North America and the West Indies during the first two decades of the century. Begun as a commercial venture, it raised money and recruited managers and laborers to engage in exploration and trade. The leading investors were rich London merchants led by Sir Thomas Smyth (active in the East India Company about 1600), others who had engaged in privateering during the war with Spain, and country gentry of small means willing to speculate while simultaneously supporting a patriotic enterprise. The charter gave the company title to the lands and resources it discovered, placed it under protection of the crown, and established orderly means for administering the enterprise in England and in Virginia.

For two decades the company poured men and money into Virginia, hoping like other trading companies to earn profits on its investment. When by 1624 it realized that its assumptions and expectations did not fit the situation, it went bankrupt. Though it had failed as a business enterprise, it was the beginning of one of England's largest and most influential settlements in America.

The company had hoped to find as much precious metals and minerals as Spain had stumbled upon. It also had intended to profit by trading with the natives. Diligent explorers hoped to reach the Indies via a passage through the North American continent. Expectations of quick riches evaporated in the face of repeated disappointments and the difficulties of survival. There were no readily accessible surface resources such as the gold and silver of Spanish America, nor did the passage to the Indies materialize; and the Virginia Indians, who barely survived under a primitive social and economic system, offered neither markets for English goods nor exports that could be sold in Europe.

The company's emphasis on exploration and trade jeopardized the venture's survival. Time and resources spent in searching for the northwest passage or digging for gold might better have been devoted to providing food and shelter. In the first seven months, famine and disease killed two-thirds of the original adventurers. Food was so scarce that men ate dogs, cats, rats, snakes, toadstools, and horsehides, and fed on the carcasses of the dead; one man killed his wife, ground her into powder, and ate her.

The company sent additional supplies but, in the long run, the settlers had to feed and clothe themselves. The iron-handed Captain John Smith, who took charge of the outpost in 1608, ruled by martial law, and forced men to work at growing food.

The realization that Virginia offered no quick road to wealth started a search for profitable staples but, since no one knew what could be raised, the company experimented with silk, wine, and iron, and in 1612, tobacco. Though tobacco eventually became the basis of Virginia's economy, at first it lacked a ready market in England. Smoking had not yet become habitual and many, including King James, regarded it as a vice. Tobacco production proved profitable but it came too late to save the company from bankruptcy. Moreover, the decision to grow staples posed new problems.

Though the company at first permitted no private enterprise, owning all land and employing the entire labor force, it experienced difficulty in making the venture profitable. There were enough settlers to dig for gold, explore, and operate a trading post but not enough to establish a settlement in the wilderness. Because the Indians were neither numerous nor willing to work for the English, additional labor had to be recruited from England. John Smith instructed the company to choose recruits carefully. Many of the first settlers were gentlemen, transients in search of quick gain, unaccustomed to hard work, and lacking in necessary skills. Virginia needed carpenters, farmers, fishermen, blacksmiths, and most of all "diggers up of trees' roots." The company sent over some children and felons as well as ninety "maidens" to meet the needs of the male population. However, it also dispatched skilled farmers who received shares of stock that entitled them to land grants after seven years of service. This arrangement increased the company's labor force only temporarily since settlers moved to their own plantations once their term of service expired.

Between 1619 and 1625, twice as many settlers arrived in Virginia as in the preceding dozen years. Recruitment of an adequate labor force, though essential for the colony's development, strained its resources. It was expensive to transport and supply new settlers whose labor did not yield immediate returns. Moreover, by 1616, the company had spent its initial capital. The London directors found ways to attract additional investment but only by renouncing some of their authority and opportunities for profit. In the end, they failed to obtain adequate financing. They wasted much capital in efforts to make quick initial gains. These failures discouraged additional investment, without which the company could not survive. It did not estimate realistically its capital needs, because it had never intended to establish a new society. The capital required to furnish a settlement with the necessities of survival—food, water, housing, government, and defense—exceeded those of an ordinary trading company. Nor could it attract sufficient additional investment by promising immediate returns.

From the start the company could not solve its administrative problems. Beginning as a trading venture and only gradually tackling the problems of settling a wilderness thousands of miles from London, it necessarily made mistakes. Many migrants died before reaching America because the ships lacked enough food and water for the voyage; and adequate housing was not available because carpenters were scarce. Nor did the company provide sufficient supplies of guns, clothing, tools, utensils, cattle, and seed, because it was ignorant of conditions in Virginia and had difficulty obtaining accurate and timely information.

The failure to earn profits led to dissension among the stockholders and officers in London. A reform group gained control in 1619 and attempted to prevent collapse. To make Virginia more attractive both to those already there and to prospective immigrants, the company abandoned martial law, granted lands to migrants, and established a local assembly composed of two representatives from each town, "hundred," or plantation. The House of Burgesses met in 1619, giving settlers a semblance of participation in decision-making, though the London authorities retained the right to approve all legislation. The company hoped to enlist greater cooperation from the colonists as well as to rely on their knowledge of local conditions to improve management.

The reforms failed. The Virginia Company could become profitable only with time. Efforts to adjust to reality came too late. An Indian massacre in 1622 killed 300 colonists and hastened the crisis. As settlers whose terms of service expired left the barracks on the company estate, and as new migrants immediately carved out private plantations, its control over the colony as well as its ability to defend it diminished. In 1624 the crown revoked the charter, making Virginia a royal colony.

The Virginia Company had modeled its enterprise on the experience of earlier English companies that had traded with developed societies in Russia, India, and the Mediterranean, and on the example of Spanish conquistadores who had seized the accumulated wealth of America's most advanced Indian civilizations. But the experiences of others was no reliable guide in

Virginia or elsewhere in North America. The company could survive only by modifying its objectives and methods and by substituting colonizing for commercial enterprise. As it did so, it found the tasks of labor recruitment, capital formation, and efficient administration well beyond its capacities. Adjustment to American conditions came too late, but the Virginia Company was England's first permanent settlement in North America.

Massachusetts

Five hundred miles north of Jamestown, a generation after Virginia's "starving time" (1608–1609), another group of Englishmen established settlements in an even more forbidding part of the North American wilderness. In one decade (1630–1640) 20,000 persons crossed the Atlantic to New England, more than double the number inhabiting Virginia after thirty years of settlement. Like the colonization of Virginia, the Great Migration to Massachusetts Bay was no ordinary business enterprise. Utilizing a royal charter as the legal basis for a new society, and the corporate form of organization as a convenient means of accomplishing its ends, the company intended to establish a permanent settlement from the outset and reckoned success not in profits but in how well it built a Zion in the Wilderness: a haven for souls stirred by new visions of God's design. New England would provide a refuge from the corruptions of Old England. Thus the Bay Company came better prepared than the Virginians to found a colony.

From the beginning it concentrated on the major problems of survival, providing food and shelter, recruiting capital and labor, and searching for crops which would sustain life, rather than looking for a passage to India or for precious metals. Hence, no conflict existed, as in Virginia, between the commercial goals of the company and the survival needs of the adventurers.

Also, the Massachusetts Bay Company tapped resources and enterprise unavailable to a trading company. Planning a permanent settlement, it realized, was expensive especially since migrants expected to stay and to maintain a living standard roughly comparable to what they had enjoyed in England. It sold shares of stock, attracting funds from both prospective emigrants and from others remaining in England yet sympathetic to its social and religious objectives. But it did not have to finance settlement entirely from its own resources. Immigrants traded possessions they could not carry abroad for what they would need in their new homes. Once in America, settlers could call upon relatives and friends at home to assist them.

The Bay colony was not only more adequately financed than Virginia was, but it also had less of a labor problem. The many settlers included persons with all the necessary social skills— ministers, lawyers, merchants, and officials as well as artisans, mechanics, shopkeepers, servants, and farmers' who were good "diggers up of trees' roots."

Possessing extensive capital and commanding large numbers of settlers, the Bay Company was also better able than its Virginia counterpart to master administrative problems. Its plan for a permanent settlement prepared it to deal with the difficulties of such an enterprise. It did not need to resort to martial law or to monopolize natural resources since it relied on voluntary cooperation. The emigrants, united by shared suffering and expectations, were eager to promote the success of an enterprise on which everybody's life and fortune depended.

For six decades Massachusetts settlers worked under the authority of the original charter as the company merged into the society it was organized to create. Its success stemmed partly from the events in England which generated extraordinary energies and passions that found an outlet in America.

The Protestant Reformation in England

Those who migrated to New England believed they had been called to participate in an event of historical importance. Their settlement, one of them proclaimed, was "as a City set upon a hill, in the open view of all the earth; the eyes of the world are upon us, because we profess ourselves to be a people in covenant with God." They believed that God had kept America hidden until the day when it would provide mankind with one last chance for regeneration and salvation.

For over 1,500 years Christianity had satisfactorily explained man's purpose and God's design to Europeans. The Church taught that men, though sinners, could choose between good and evil and hence each man determined his own fate— whether he would enjoy eternal life after death or suffer the eternal torments of Hell. The Church offered men models of holiness in the monasteries and rituals of worship in the churches. A Christian who observed God's commands, performed good works, kept his faith, and received absolution for his sins, expected to be saved.

By the sixteenth century, however, many Christians found their faith waning, their inner lives in turmoil. The Church's paths to salvation failed to bring spiritual peace. Fearing damnation, people looked for a new gospel of deliverance. It came in 1517. Martin Luther, a German Augustinian monk, denounced the pope and Church doctrines, thus touching off the Protestant Reformation. Luther received support from some German princes jealous of funds drained from their territories by Rome, and eager to strengthen themselves by appropriating the Church's wealth and power. Though the Protestant revolt could not have succeeded without such mundane political support, it spread rapidly, enlisting popular support among pious Christians alienated by the then notorious corruption within a church, supposedly universal but actually dominated by Italian politicians. Luther's message spread mainly, however, because thousands of Christians, like Luther himself, no longer found in Roman Catholicism an adequate interpretation of experience or a suitable guide to their lives.

The emergence of a modern social order involved not only the creation of powerful nation states and the increasing commercialization of the economic system but also the formulation of new beliefs and codes of behavior. Protestantism attempted to supply an ideology that would sustain people through the break up of an old social order and the painful emergence of a new one.

In England as on the Continent, Protestantism prospered, backed by the crown. The kingdom was growing richer, yet life seemed more uncertain; no one could be sure of the future. Life had once been more secure, even if the aspirations of most people were limited. Fewer opportunities for improvement had existed but there had been less danger of sinking below one's inherited station. But now England was changing. New economic opportunities enabled some to rise, though others were pushed off the land or speculated unsuccessfully in the commercial arena.

People in motion searched for ways to stabilize their lives. The unfortunate craved consolation and protection; the successful feared that fortune would turn against them. Those most afflicted by uncertainty were the groups somewhere in the middle of the social structure—farmers who owned some land, merchants on the way up, professional men who had positions to lose and expectations that might be frustrated in a society experiencing greater upward and downward mobility than in the past. Their life style distinguished them from the lower and higher classes whose positions were more firmly fixed and who consequently experienced less anxiety than those with more unpredictable futures.

The middling elements were self-conscious and individualistic. Better educated and more independent than most Englishmen, they actively tried to shape their lives, believing that men were not prisoners of fate but determined their own success or failure. Experience taught them that success stemmed from virtue, the capacity to work hard, save, and to seize economic opportunities. Yet men often found themselves unable to control the forces that shaped their lives. They turned for help and relief to the church and to the state but neither responded adequately.

Catholicism urged men to scorn the flesh in favor of other-worldly self-denial, but in practice tolerated worldliness among laity and clergy, offering sinners quick and easy absolution. Moreover, the faith was profoundly anti-individualistic. It encouraged acceptance and resignation since what counted was rebirth after death and it insisted that men approach God by rejecting the world. Though the Church acknowledged man's free will, it offered convenient intercession in case an individual's godly impulses proved too weak.

Little of this suited the needs of those perplexed by early modern society. These men were drawn to a faith which regarded sin not as a force pervading the world, a part of the air men breathe, but the result of an individual act. To find salvation, each man, whatever his calling, must actively strive for deliverance in the workaday world. No church or priest, no elaborate ritual, could relieve men of their personal responsibilities. John Calvin, a Swiss theologian, formulated a doctrine which claimed to recover an earlier, purer Christian faith and which powerfully appealed to men of his own day. Calvinism spread across Europe and into England where those who hoped to purify the Anglican church of Roman error embraced it.

English Puritans believed that man's original sin had left him totally depraved. All men were born with an irresistible propensity for evil: "In Adam's fall, we sinned all," Puritans taught their children. Since each child inherited this curse, man was incapable of saving himself. Neither good works, confession of sin, faithful church attendance, nor intercession by the clergy could offer redemption.

Man's only hope was faith. God had already picked His Saints, those He had chosen to save. Men wondered whether they were among the elect and waited for signs—an overpowering inner experience that told them they were among the regenerate. Though man could not will to be saved, he could strive to lead a godly life, an indication though not a certainty of sanctification. Good works did not save souls, but since Christian virtues expressed love of God they were a possible sign of election. Those who led model lives suspected that their ability to resist temptation better than most men derived from God's grace. But no one could ever be sure. Signs of salvation reassured men only of probable election for eternal life. Conversion thus became the Calvinist's preoccupying concern.

The new faith sanctified each man's calling, since every person had the same obligation and the same chance. Neither the priesthood nor the monastery offered an advantage. Because one could never be certain of salvation, an endless search for signs of grace, revealed by the capacity to act morally, imposed upon the Calvinist far greater internal discipline than the external rewards and punishments of the Catholic church. And with the denial of absolution from sin, compromises with evil could no longer be tolerated. This redefinition of the Christian pilgrimage offered no easy path, but at least it seemed to conform more closely to human experience and to satisfy the needs of changing conditions. "You must not think to go to heaven in a feather bed," Calvinists learned, because "if you will be Christ's disciples, you must take up his cross and it will make you sweat."

English Puritans, like Calvinists on the Continent, demanded a church reformation in line with these new doctrines. Since they believed in individual salvation, the role of the priesthood and the church changed. The church could neither absolve men of their sins nor save them; it could, however, preach the gospel and help men find signs of salvation. Elaborate rituals and lavish ceremony, architectural splendor and traditional worship, all departed from the simplicity of early Christianity. The Bible was the Christian's ultimate source of God's word; no pope or bishop, no prince or king took precedence over man's direct relationship with God or had the right to intervene.

This included the English monarchy. The Tudors had broken with Rome for political, not theological, reasons. Henry VIII substituted himself for the pope as head of the Church of England but he did not radically alter Catholic practices. Queen Elizabeth also wished to avoid alienating traditionalists but her precarious hold on the throne, early in her reign, forced half-hearted concessions to Calvinists. During the reign of her successor, James I (1603–1625), Puritans demanded abolition of hierarchy in the church, giving each congregation the right to govern its own spiritual affairs. They also insisted on "purifying" or simplifying church ritual and worship. The crown refused, fearful of turmoil and loss of control over an institution whose power and resources supported the dynasty.

James was the first member of the new Stuart dynasty and, like his successors, he tried to make the crown truly sovereign. Whatever stood in the way—an uncooperative Parliament or religious dissenters—had to be crushed. His son, Charles I (1625–1649), continued his father's quest for absolute power. When Parliament balked, Charles ruled without it for over ten years (1629–1641), taxing his subjects by decree rather than consent. Puritans had fought the crown in Parliament, in alliance with other disaffected groups, and they relentlessly pressed for reformation of the Church of England. Intent on crushing opposition, Charles appointed William Laud as Archbishop of Canterbury to wipe out religious dissent. Laud forced Calvinist clergy from their pulpits, required congregations to conform, imprisoned and tortured Puritan leaders and suppressed their publications.

Puritan hopes had rested on the assumption that the Church of England could be captured from within. But widespread official persecution dimmed such hopes. A generation earlier, a Puritan congregation in Nottinghamshire, despairing of success, separated from the Anglican church and moved to Holland in 1608 seeking religious freedom. After a decade abroad, they decided to move again, fearful that further residence in the Netherlands would jeopardize the group's survival as English Calvinists. With a patent from the Virginia Company and financial support from England, the Pilgrims sailed to America on the *Mayflower* in 1620 and settled at Plymouth, Massachusetts, near Cape Cod.

During the decade that the Plymouth colony was gaining a foothold many more English Calvinists became progressively more disheartened. Persecution caused increasing numbers to see no future within the Church of England, no escape from it except by migration. A depression that pressed hard on the centers of the cloth industry where Puritanism had many adherents added to the discontent and swelled the number of potential migrants.

The City Upon a Hill

For several years the Puritans—ministers, country gentry, and merchants—thought of establishing a settlement in New England that would be both a commercial base for fishing and a refuge. After several false starts, they succeeded in 1629 when the king chartered the Massachusetts Bay Company. That same year twelve Puritan members of the company signed the Cambridge Agreement, declaring their intention to emigrate to America. They took with them the charter and with it the power to govern, thereby hoping to protect themselves against the crown or other outside control.

Eleven ships sailed in 1630. Settlement started in Boston and Salem and a new society began to take shape. The charter called for a governor and assistants chosen by the freemen. These were the stockholders, but since there were only twelve among the original settlers it was necessary to elect others to freemanship. However, the first governor, John Winthrop, lawyer and country squire, and a leader of the group that launched the company, sought to preserve tight control over the settlement. In violation of the charter, he declared only church members eligible for freemanship, on the assumption that only the godly could be entrusted with power. Winthrop and his supporters also ignored the charter provisions that gave freemen the right to choose their governor and enact company—and hence colony—law. In 1632, one town objected to a tax levied by the assistants and after that the freemen regained the power to elect the governor and to choose deputies from each town to the General Court, or legislature. An elite ran the colony's politics, but without permanent tenure in office, and with its decisions subject to review. The Puritans thus attempted to balance the claims of individual freedom and the need for communal order. Only animals had natural liberty, John Winthrop reminded the people, the freedom to do whatever impulse dictated. Men who enjoyed the blessing of civic liberty in a covenanted community were free only to obey the righteous commands of godly authority as interpreted by upright rulers. Yet Winthrop, who served as governor for eleven years, was several times ousted from office by disgruntled freemen and rival leaders. In Massachusetts, as in Virginia, settlers resented efforts by a few to monopolize power and they demanded the right to participate in decision-making. Though the notion that government derived its power from the consent of the governed was foreign to this generation's thinking, people insisted that power be exercised responsibly. Tyranny would not be permitted. Rulers were bound to govern *under* law as faithfully as the ruled were obliged to obey authority.

The township dominated communal life in Massachusetts. Each group of settlers petitioned the General Court for land on which to establish a community. The town leaders then distributed it, in amounts according to the social status of the inhabitants. Local officials were chosen, village lots and roads laid out, and a church erected. In contrast with Virginia where individuals settled wherever they pleased, Puritans established and maintained well-regulated communities which enforced conformity to the Bay colony's rules.

In a colony committed to a religious ideal, the church proved a powerful source of discipline. Groups often migrated under the leadership of a minister who petitioned the General Court for a town charter and provided firm leadership in the early years of town building. Though Puritans asserted that they remained in communion with the Church of England, once free to do as they wanted, they organized their own kind of church life. Each congregation chose its own minister and adopted a confession of faith and style of worship in accordance with its interpretation of Calvinist teaching, although synods composed of neighboring churches, coordinated congregations. Every inhabitant had to attend services, support the church, and accept its discipline though only the elect, those who had experienced God's grace, were technically church "members." Every European became a church member at birth, but the Congregational churches in New England were select bodies, made up exclusively of "Saints" with full and exclusive power to run the church as they saw fit. These unplanned changes came about because Puritans in a wilderness were free to pursue the logic of their beliefs. They insisted, however, that their new model churches remain part of the Anglican communion.

Despite the importance of the church and the power of the ministers, the Bay colony was not a theocracy. Although freemen had to be church members, the clergy did not rule or generally hold office. However, laymen exercised political power in consultation with the ministers. John Winthrop and his fellow leaders made no distinction between the sacred and the secular; God ruled over every aspect of human affairs. Heresy was as much a crime against the state as theft or murder.

Yet men did not live by faith alone, not even Puritans. The colony supplied its material needs by raising food, and by trading furs, fish, and timber to finance imports from England. Though settlers had to work hard at their tasks, merchants were expected to charge "just" prices and artisans to receive "just" wages. Excessive pursuit of wealth marked one as a victim of the devil's snares and made one subject to punishment.

Begun as a community in covenant with God, the Bay colony successfully parried a series of dangers that threatened its success. The most formidable came neither from the Indian wars, nor the attacks on the charter in England, but from internal dissension. Puritans were united in their spiritual commitment but men sometimes interpreted the Almighty's design differently.

Early in 1635 the town of Salem chose a new pastor, Roger Williams, a Cambridge University graduate who had migrated four years earlier. Williams soon stated publicly that the colony charter was void because the crown could not grant land belonging to the Indians. He considered the colony's invasion of the rights of conscience even worse, and argued that the church should exclude the unregenerate since their presence compromised the purity of the faith. Forced worship stank in God's and Williams' nostrils. As long as the community imposed orthodoxy, good Christians might be forced to accept erroneous doctrines promulgated by the church and enforced by the state. Each man, Williams believed, was a church unto himself, seeking God throughout his life. Since the search never ends, men must be free to follow wherever conscience leads, for there was no other path to God.

Williams challenged the foundations of the Massachusetts experiment. Most Puritans believed they had discovered the Truth and hence it was their duty to uproot error before it spread. Winthrop and others insisted that the magistrates had a responsibility to reclaim those who strayed and to prevent them from infecting others. Consequently, the Massachusetts General Court banished Roger Williams in September, 1635. During the winter he fled Boston, taking refuge among the Indians from whom he purchased land on which he founded the city of Providence. Williams later obtained a royal charter for the Rhode Island colony and granted freedom of conscience to all.

Like Williams, Anne Hutchinson also threatened the authority of the church and magistrates and the survival of the Bible Commonwealth in Massachusetts. Uncertain of her own election, Mistress Anne claimed that God spoke to her directly. The revelation brought her peace and spread the word that the only valid sign of election was a mystical experience. She denied that outward godly behavior was a reliable indication of one's inner condition since one could easily play the pious hypocrite. But if each individual relied exclusively on mystical experience, neither the church nor the state could enforce uniform standards of behavior. A thousand heresies would spring forth from a thousand mystics and if good works were no sign of election, people would have little incentive to behave morally.

Hutchinson was a greater threat than Williams because she found powerful support in Boston. Once again John Winthrop mobilized the forces of orthodoxy. The General Court convicted Hutchinson of sedition and banished her and another follower. Together with her husband and children, she found temporary refuge in Roger Williams' new settlement. She was later murdered by Indians.

The Williams and Hutchinson cases revealed the precariousness of a covenanted community in the face of individual interpretations of God's intent. Without firm control by an elite, John Winthrop and others feared that the City on a Hill might disintegrate into a hundred petty sects each with its own vision of a Wilderness Zion. So persistent were the disruptive tendencies within Massachusetts Puritanism, that six years after the first settlement, a group of orthodox Calvinists in several towns around Boston, led by Thomas Hooker, one of the colony's leading preachers, moved to Connecticut. Hooker and his followers claimed they wanted more room in which to settle but they also sought freedom from the rulers of Massachusetts who, they believed, governed with too little regard for the wishes of the majority as required by the charter. In 1639 the Connecticut migrants adopted the Fundamental Orders, a charter they hoped would legalize their settlement and define its terms of government. As in Massachusetts, towns elected deputies to an assembly but freemen need not be church members, and the magistrates had less freedom of action. These modifications had religious origins but political repercussions. Hooker believed that since one could never be sure that those claiming to be regenerate had indeed received grace, they should not exercise too much power. The magistrates' powers should therefore be restricted. In 1662, the sixteen towns of Connecticut received a royal charter legitimatizing the authority assumed by the colonizing generation.

The Virgina company measured success in terms of return on investment. The New England Puritans judged their efforts by how close they came to building a godly community. But even before the passing of the first generation of Saints, some began to doubt that man could escape the past in the New World. Toward the end of his long life, Roger Williams warned John Winthrop, Jr., son of his great antagonist: "Sir, when we that have been the eldest and are rotting a generation will act, I fear, far unlike the first Winthrops and their Models of Christian Charity: I fear that the common trinity of the world—Profit, Preferment, Pleasure—will be here as in all the world besides:

that Prelacy and Popery too will in this wilderness predominate; and that God Land will be as great a God with us English as God Gold was with the Spaniard." Only time would test the accuracy of Williams' prophesy.

Maryland

In addition to the chartered trading company, the English had another flexible instrument of overseas expansion, the proprietary grant. Maryland was the first of the proprietary colonies and its founding illustrates an alternate method of English expansion.

The joint-stock company appealed most strongly to merchants seeking overseas opportunities; the proprietary attracted aristocrats and politicians with close ties to the crown who saw in landed estates a means of increasing their wealth. In 1632, the crown made Cecilius Calvert, 2nd Lord Baltimore, proprietor of Maryland, a colony carved out of land formerly held by the Virginia Company. Calvert's father was a Caltholic and a faithful servant of James I. That monarch's son, Charles I, rewarded the Baltimore family with extensive territory in America.

The proprietor had had tremendous authority in the past. The English crown had granted special privileges to noblemen willing to subdue the rebellious Scots and Welsh. These grants were models for later proprietary charters. Lord Baltimore owned all the land in Maryland, controlled its government, and sought to develop his colony as a great manorial estate. Expecting to profit principally from the land, the proprietor reserved 12,000 acres in each county and established manors to be farmed by tenants, granted manors of 1,000 to 3,000 acres to others, and sold small farms to freeholders who paid a modest yearly rent. The proprietor also had the power to tax, command the militia, and establish courts and an assembly, though he retained the ultimate power to make and enforce law. Secondarily, the Baltimore family also intended Maryland to become a shelter for fellow Catholics seeking refuge from persecution at home.

Medieval feudal arrangements, strongly influenced the colonization design for Maryland. The first settlers, mostly craftsmen, servants, and farmers, were better prepared than those in Virginia and thus escaped a "starving time." As Maryland grew and proprietary authority weakened, the original settlement plan needed modification. As long as people could obtain land elsewhere without accepting manorial obligations, Maryland could not compete for new migrants. The small farm, raising tobacco and food, not the manorial estate, predominated. The proprietor never used his right to establish manorial courts. As in Virginia, counties and hundreds administered themselves. Despite the proprietor's legal monopoly of political power, he found it convenient to create an assembly and concede it a voice in decision-making.

Nor did Maryland become a Catholic settlement. Since few English Catholics were willing to migrate most of the settlers were Protestant.

Profitable settlement by Protestant farmers coupled with a declared haven for Catholics meant that both groups would enjoy religious tolerance. Expediency, not principle, led to the Toleration Act (1649) which granted religious freedom to Maryland Christians. (Jews did not share in the blessing.) The Baltimores' economic interests led them to modify policies even at the expense of rights and authority granted in the original charter. As in Virginia and Massachusetts, colonizers soon learned that success in the New World placed a premium on the ability to adapt to new conditions.

From New Hampshire to Georgia

In the century following the birth of Maryland, nine other English colonies completed the foundations of English settlement in North America. Most were proprietaries and except for Georgia they were established between 1660 and 1680. The popularity of the proprietary reflected the growing regard of English landed interests for America's virgin lands, which, properly developed, offered generous opportunities for profit. By relying on settlers themselves to supply most of the initial developmental capital, proprietors did not need to invest much of their own money. Since they risked only small amounts and had no stockholders to please or fear, they were willing to wait until they could sell land to immigrants for annual rents or until real estate values rose.

England acquired New York and New Jersey from the Dutch, then a powerful maritime and commercial rival whom the British fought several times during the middle of the seventeenth century. In 1623 the Dutch West India Company established a permanent settlement in New Amsterdam to trade in furs. The English seized the Dutch forts in 1664 and the king granted his brother, the Duke of York (later James II) extensive proprietary powers. The duke hoped to profit from New York, and treated the conquered Dutch liberally, permitting religious freedom, and eventually granting freeholders an assembly. When the duke was crowned King James II, New York became a royal colony. In 1664, the duke granted New Jersey to proprietors but the crown regained control in 1702.

The well-connected nobility also founded the Carolinas. In 1663 a group with close ties to the crown and strong overseas interests received a charter. They invested little capital, expecting migrants to come from older colonies such as Virginia, the British West Indies, and Europe. In 1669, the proprietors issued the Fundamental Constitutions mapping out an aristocratic social structure for the Carolinas. A hereditary aristocracy would receive 40 percent of the land in each county. The scheme proved unworkable since manorial estates without tenants to work them had little value. The Carolinas faced difficulties enough attracting settlers without discouraging land hungry farmers by the prospect of working another man's estate. Instead, the proprietors, like those elsewhere, found it necessary to sell freeholds to farmers, who paid annual rent, grant them religious freedom, and establish an assembly. As Carolina grew, the proprietors had constant difficulty governing. In 1721 South

Carolina became a royal colony as did North Carolina in 1729 when the proprietors finally sold their claims to the crown.

The impulses behind the founding of Pennsylvania combined the religious zeal that inspired the New England settlement with the personal interests of a proprietary family. William Penn, the son of an admiral to whom Charles II was financially indebted, rejected an easy aristocratic life. The young Penn became a Quaker, spreading the faith energetically, suffering temporary imprisonment in the Tower of London. The king discharged his debts to the Penns by granting William a large tract that became Pennsylvania. In 1682, he also acquired the nearby Delaware territory from the Duke of York.

Penn's offer of religious freedom and land on liberal terms attracted Quakers from England, Wales, Ireland, and Germany. He assumed a paternalistic attitude toward the well-being of the colony but did not anticipate that immigrants whom he treated generously would insist on a substantial voice in governing Pennsylvania. As proprietor, Penn controlled the land, appointed the governor, and established an assembly chosen by freeholders. Under constant pressure from settlers during the first twenty years, he finally granted the assembly the power to initiate laws, though he had originally created it as an advisory body. As Pennsylvania prospered, populated by a variety of ethnic and religious elements, a powerful native Quaker elite emerged that competed with the Penn family for control. Penn governed neighboring Delaware through the same authority that controlled Pennsylvania until 1701 when the small colony established its own assembly though a single governor chosen by the proprietor ruled.

Georgia, the last colony established during the colonial period, originated in humanitarian impulses that shaped a noble colonizing purpose thoroughly inappropriate to American conditions. James E. Oglethorpe led a group of prominent individuals who thought a new settlement in America could absorb thousands of the English poor. Though settling people abroad would be costly, the trustees of Georgia, chartered in 1732, expected that the colony would soon become self-supporting. Hard-working Georgia farmers would no longer be public charges as they were in England. Moreover, Georgia would strengthen the Southern defenses of the American colonies against the Spaniards in Florida and would produce silk for export to Britain to lessen dependence on foreign sources.

The key to success, the trustees thought, lay in transforming shiftless people into enterprising yeomen by controlled development. Since the settlers were too poor to finance migration and settlement, the trustees, with generous support from Parliament, provided the capital. To make Georgia easily defensible against the Spaniards, settlements were compact and population relatively dense. Hence farms remained small, and to prevent speculation and dispersal of migrants, land could neither be alienated nor sold. The trustees also barred Negro slaves for fear that whites would prefer to import them rather than work themselves, and that availability of slaves would attract speculative and absentee landowners. To discourage production of staples such as tobacco and rice which had proved profitable elsewhere, Georgia farmers had to grow silk to validate their claims. Finally by prohibiting alcohol, the trustees expected to promote sobriety and discourage indolence.

After twenty years, the trustees abandoned the noble experiment. Their rigid controls discouraged migration and private investment. Military obligations antagonized the farmers. Also, they could not expand their lands or sell them, and had little incentive to work hard. Moreover, silk production soon proved impractical. Without representative institutions, a bureaucracy that was at best paternalistic, and sometimes corrupt and arbitrary, governed Georgia. The company attempted to rescue the scheme from failure by allowing farmers slaves and liquor, and the right to pass on their properties to their heirs. Settlers bitterly complained that "the poor inhabitants of Georgia are scattered over the face of the earth; her plantations a wild; her towns a desert; her villages in rubbish; her improvements a byword, and her liberties a jest; an object of pity to friends and of insult, contempt and ridicule to enemies." In 1752 the crown took control and Georgia became another royal colony rather than a humanitarian refuge for England's poor.

During the century-and-a-quarter between the founding of Virginia and the establishment of Georgia (1607–1732), English colonizers discovered that settlements planned at home often had to be modified abroad. None could predict that the wilderness would force men to abandon preconceptions and adjust to strange and often threatening circumstances. An English trading company became a permanent settlement, producing tobacco; another joint-stock company established a City on a Hill only to find that distance from kings and bishops did not eliminate dangers threatening a Christian commonwealth. And proprietary grants to noblemen with feudal intentions had to be modified in the face of laborers, short in supply but long in demands for land of their own and increased political and religious liberties. The long term growth and prosperity of each settlement depended on the ability of the founding generation to grapple intelligently and practically with the difficulties of setting up new societies. None was more important than developing a productive system for profitably exploiting America's resources.

Document: The Pilgrim Experience
William Bradford's History of the Pilgrims

Born into a family of yeomen farmers in Yorkshire, England, in 1589 William Bradford was preoccupied from youth with the fate of his soul. At an early age he was attending the sermons of Puritan preachers and later joined a separatist congregation which renounced the Church of England. The reason for separating are recounted below in Bradford's History of the

Source: William Bradford, *Of Plymouth Plantation, 1620–1647*, ed., S. E. Morison (New York, 1966), pp. 6–10, 23–27, 47, 58–63, 75–79, 84, 316–317, 320, 321, 333–334, 236.

<u>Pilgrims</u>, *those Puritans who abandoned not only the Anglican church but their homeland, first for Holland, then for the New World so they could worship God according to the true faith as they understood it. Bradford became a leader of the migration and a year after the Pilgrims settled in Massachusetts, he became governor, an office he held for thirty years.*

Bradford's account is a moving epic which vividly conveys in simple, eloquent biblical language the intense religious faith that stirred the minds and hearts of the Pilgrims. Bradford summed up his life and that of his generation in these simple lines:

> *From my years young in days of youth*
> *God did make known to me His truth*
> *And call'd me from my native place*
> *For to enjoy the means of grace.*
> *In wilderness he did me guide,*
> *And in strange lands for me provide*
> *In fears and wants, through weal and woe,*
> *A Pilgrim passed I to and fro.*

(Origin of the Pilgrim Church in England, 1550–1607)

. . . The one side laboured to have the right worship of God and discipline of Christ established in the church, according to the simplicity of the gospel, without the mixture of men's inventions; and to have and to be ruled by the laws of God's Word, dispensed in those offices, and by those officers of Pastors, Teachers and Elders, etc. according to the Scriptures. The other party, though under many colours and pretences, endeavoured to have the episcopal dignity (after the popish manner) with their large power and jurisdiction still retained; with all those courts, canons and ceremonies, together with all such livings, revenues and subordinate officers, with other such means as formerly upheld their antichristian greatness and enabled them with lordly and tyrannous power to persecute the poor servants of God. This contention was so great, as neither the honour of

God, the common persecution, nor the mediation of Mr. Calvin and other worthies of the Lord in those places, could prevail with those thus episcopally minded; but they proceeded by all means to disturb the peace of this poor persecuted church, even so far as to charge (very unjustly and ungodlily yet prelatelike) some of their chief opposers with rebellion and high treason against the Emperor, and other such crimes.

And this contention died not with Queen Mary, nor was left beyond the seas. But at her death these people returning into England under gracious Queen Elizabeth, many of them being preferred to bishoprics and other promotions according to their aims and desires, that inveterate hatred against the holy discipline of Christ in His church[1] hath continued to this day. Insomuch that for fear it should prevail, all plots and devices have been used to keep it out, incensing the Queen and State against it as dangerous for the commonwealth; and that it was most needful that the fundamental points of religion should be preached in those ignorant and superstitious times. And to win the weak and ignorant they might retain divers harmless ceremonies; and though it were to be wished that divers things were reformed, yet this was not a season for it. And many the like, to stop the mouths of the more godly, to bring them on to yield to one ceremony after another, and one corruption after another; by these wiles beguiling some and corrupting others till at length they began to persecute all the zealous professors in the land (though they knew little what this discipline meant) both by word and deed, if they would not submit to their ceremonies and become slaves to them and their popish trash, which have no ground in the Word of God, but are relics of that man of sin. And the more the light of the gospel grew, the more they urged their subscriptions to these corruptions. So as (notwithstanding all their former pretences and fair colours) they whose eyes God had not justly blinded might easily see whereto these things tended. And to cast contempt the more upon the sincere servants

---

[1] Bradford means the Congregational discipline. His account of church history during Elizabeth's reign is of course a partisan one, unfair to the acts and motives of everyone not in the left wing of Protestantism.

of God, they opprobriously and most injuriously gave unto and imposed upon them that name of Puritans, which is said the Novatians out of pride did assume and take unto themselves. And lamentable it is to see the effects which have followed. Religion hath been disgraced, the godly grieved, afflicted, persecuted, and many exiled; sundry have lost their lives in prisons and other ways. On the other hand, sin hath been countenanced; ignorance, profaneness and atheism increased, and the papists encouraged to hope again for a day.

This made that holy man Mr. Perkins cry out in his exhortation to repentance, upon Zephaniah ii:

> Religion (saith he) hath been amongst us this thirty-five years; but the more it is published, the more it is contemned and reproached of many, etc. Thus not profaneness nor wickedness but religion itself is a byword, a mockingstock, and a matter of reproach; so that in England at this day the man or woman that begins to profess religion and to serve God, must resolve with himself to sustain mocks and injuries even as though he lived amongst the enemies of religion.

And this, common experience hath confirmed and made too apparent. But that I may come more near my intendment.

When as by the travail and diligence of some godly and zealous preachers, and God's blessing on their labours, as in other places of the land, so in the North parts, many became enlightened by the Word of God and had their ignorance and sins discovered unto them, and began by His grace to reform their lives and make conscience of their ways; the work of God was no sooner manifest in them but presently they were both scoffed and scorned by the profane multitude; and the ministers urged with the yoke of subscription, or else must be silenced. And the poor people were so vexed with apparitors and pursuivants[2] and the commissary courts, as truly their affliction was not small. Which, notwithstanding, they bore sundry years with much patience, till they were occasioned by the continuance and increase

---

[2] Officers of the Church of England whose duty was to enforce conformity.

of these troubles, and other means which the Lord raised up in those days, to see further into things by the light of the Word of God. How not only these base and beggarly ceremonies were unlawful, but also that the lordly and tyrannous power of the prelates ought not to be submitted unto; which thus, contrary to the freedom of the gospel, would load and burden men's consciences and by their compulsive power make a profane mixture of persons and things in the worship of God. And that their offices and callings, courts and canons, etc. were unlawful and antichristian; being such as have no warrant in the Word of God, but the same that were used in popery and still retained. Of which a famous author thus writeth in his Dutch commentaries, at the coming of King James into England:

> The new king (saith he) found there established the reformed religion according to the reformed religion of King Edward VI, retaining or keeping still the spiritual state of the bishops, etc. after the old manner, much varying and differing from the reformed churches in Scotland, France and the Netherlands, Emden, Geneva, etc., whose reformation is cut, or shapen much nearer the first Christian churches, as it was used in the Apostles' times.

So many, therefore, of these professors as saw the evil of these things in these parts, and whose hearts the Lord had touched with heavenly zeal for His truth, they shook off this yoke of antichristian bondage, and as the Lord's free people joined themselves (by a covenant of the Lord) into a church estate, in the fellowship of the gospel, to walk in all His ways made known, or to be made known unto them, according to their best endeavours, whatsoever it should cost them, the Lord assisting them. And that it cost them something this ensuing history will declare.

These people became two distinct bodies or churches, and in regard of distance of place did congregate severally; for they were of sundry towns and villages, some in Nottinghamshire, some of Lincolnshire, and some of Yorkshire where they border nearest together. In one of these churches (besides others of note) was Mr. John Smith,[3] a man of able gifts and a good preacher, who afterwards was chosen their pastor. But these afterwards falling into some errours in the Low Countries, there (for the most part) buried themselves and their names.

But in this other church (which must be the subject of our discourse) besides other worthy men, was Mr. Richard Clyfton, a grave and reverend preacher, who by his pains and diligence had done much good, and under God had been a means of the conversion of many. And also that famous and worthy man Mr. John Robinson, who afterwards was their pastor for many years, till the Lord took him away by death. Also Mr. William Brewster a reverend man, who afterwards was chosen an elder of the church and lived with them till old age.

But after these things they could not long continue in any peaceable condition, but were hunted and persecuted on every side, so as their former afflictions were but as flea-bitings in comparison of these which now came upon them. For some were taken and clapped up in prison, others had their houses beset and watched night and day, and hardly escaped their hands; and the most were fain to flee and leave their houses and habitations, and the means of their livelihood.

Yet these and many other sharper things which afterward befell them, were no other than they looked for, and therefore were the better prepared to bear them by the assistance of God's grace and Spirit.

Yet seeing themselves thus molested, and that there was no hope of their continuance there, by a joint consent they resolved to go into the Low Countries, where they heard was freedom of religion for all men; as also how sundry from London and other parts of the land had been exiled and persecuted for the same cause, and were gone thither, and lived at Amsterdam and in other places of the land. So after they had continued together about a year, and kept their meetings every Sabbath in one

[3] An alumnus of Christ's College, Cambridge, who seceded from the Church of England in 1605 and preached to the Separatist church at Gainsborough. This congregation emigrated in 1608 to Amsterdam, where Smith embraced a number of strange opinions and his church broke up.

place or other, exercising the worship of God amongst themselves, notwithstanding all the diligence and malice of their adversaries, they seeing they could no longer continue in that condition, they resolved to get over into Holland as they could. Which was in the year 1607 and 1608; of which more at large in the next chapter. . . .

(Reasons for Leaving Holland)

After they had lived in this city [Amsterdam] about some eleven or twelve years (which is the more observable being the whole time of that famous truce between that state and the Spaniards) and sundry of them were taken away by death and many others began to be well stricken in years (the grave mistress of Experience having taught them many things), those prudent governors with sundry of the sagest members began both deeply to apprehend their present dangers and wisely to foresee the future and think of timely remedy. In the agitation of their thoughts, and much discourse of things hereabout, at length they began to incline to this conclusion: of removal to some other place. Not out of any newfangledness or other such like giddy humor by which men are oftentimes transported to their great hurt and danger, but for sundry weighty and solid reasons, some of the chief of which I will here briefly touch.

And first, they saw and found by experience the hardness of the place and country to be such as few in comparison would come to them, and fewer that would bide it out and continue with them. For many that came to them, and many more that desired to be with them, could not endure that great labour and hard fare, with other inconveniences which they underwent and were contented with. But though they loved their persons, approved their cause and honoured their sufferings, yet they left them as it were weeping, as Orpah did her mother-in-law Naomi, or as those Romans did Cato in Utica who desired to be excused and borne with, though they could not all be Catos. For many, though they desired to enjoy the ordinances of God in their purity and the liberty of the gospel with them, yet (alas) they admitted of bondage with danger of conscience, rather than to endure these hardships. Yea, some preferred and chose the prisons in England rather than this liberty in Holland with these afflictions. But it was thought that if a better and easier place of living could be had, it would draw many and take away these discouragements. Yea, their pastor would often say that many of those who both wrote and preached now against them, if they were in a place where they might have liberty and live comfortably, they would then practice as they did.

Secondly. They saw that though the people generally bore all these difficulties very cheerfully and with a resolute courage, being in the best and strength of their years; yet old age began to steal on many of them; and their great and continual labours, with other crosses and sorrows, hastened it before the time. So as it was not only probably thought, but apparently seen, that within a few years more they would be in danger to scatter, by necessities pressing them, or sink under their burdens, or both. And therefore according to the divine proverb, that a wise man seeth the plague when it cometh, and hideth himself, Proverbs xxii. 3, so they like skillful and beaten soldiers were fearful either to be entrapped or surrounded by their enemies so as they should neither be able to fight nor fly. And therefore thought it better to dislodge betimes to some place of better advantage and less danger, if any such could be found.

Thirdly. As necessity was a taskmaster over them so they were forced to be such, not only to their servants but in a sort to their dearest children, the which as it did not a little wound the tender hearts of many a loving father and mother, so it produced likewise sundry sad and sorrowful effects. For many of their children that were of best dispositions and gracious inclinations, having learned to bear the yoke in their youth and willing to bear part of their parents' burden, were oftentimes so oppressed with their heavy labours that though their minds were free and willing, yet their bodies bowed under the weight of the same, and became decrepit in their early youth, the vigour of nature being consumed in the very bud as it were. But that which was more lamentable, and of all sorrows most heavy to be borne, was that many of their children, by these occasions and the great licentiousness of youth in that country, and the manifold temptations of the place, were drawn away by evil examples into extravagant and dangerous courses, getting the reins off their necks and departing from their parents. Some became soldiers, others took upon them far voyages by sea, and others some worse courses tending to dissoluteness and the danger of their souls, to the great grief of their parents and dishonour of God. So that they saw their posterity would be in danger to degenerate and be corrupted.

Lastly (and which was not least), a great hope and inward zeal they had of laying some good foundation, or at least to make some way thereunto, for the propagating and advancing the gospel of the kingdom of Christ in those remote parts of the world; yea, though they should be but even as stepping-stones unto others for the performing of so great a work.

These and some other like reasons moved them to undertake this resolution of their removal; the which they afterward prosecuted with so great difficulties, as by the sequel will appear.

The place they had thoughts on was some of those vast and unpeopled countries of America, which are fruitful and fit for habitation, being devoid of all civil inhabitants, where there are only savage and brutish men which range up and down, little otherwise than the wild beasts of the same. This proposition being made public and coming to the scanning of all, it raised many variable opinions amongst men and caused many fears and doubts amongst themselves. Some, from their reasons and hopes conceived, laboured to stir up and encourage the rest to undertake and prosecute the same; others again, out of their fears, objected against it and sought to divert from it; alleging many things, and those neither unreasonable nor unprobable; as that it was a great design and subject to many unconceivable perils and dangers; as, besides the casualties of the sea (which none can be freed from), the length of the voyage was such as the weak bodies of women and other persons worn out with age and travail (as many of them were) could never be able to endure. And yet if they should, the miseries of the land which they should be exposed unto, would be too hard to be borne and likely, some or all of them together, to consume and utterly to ruinate them. For there they should be liable to famine and nakedness and the want, in a manner, of all things. The change of air, diet and drinking of water would infect their bodies with sore sicknesses and grievous diseases. And also those which should escape or overcome these difficulties should yet be in continual danger of the savage people, who are cruel, barbarous and most treacherous, being most furious in their rage and merciless where they overcome; not being content only to kill and take away life, but delight to torment men in the most bloody manner that may be; flaying some alive with the shells of fishes, cutting off the members and joints of others by piecemeal and broiling on the coals, eat the collops of their flesh in their sight whilst they live, with other cruelties horrible to be related.

And surely it could not be thought but the very hearing of these things could not but move the very bowels of men to grate within them and make the weak to quake and tremble. It was further objected that it would require greater sums of money to furnish such a voyage and to fit them with necessaries, than their consumed estates would amount to; and yet they must as well look to be seconded with supplies as presently to be transported. Also many precedents of ill success and lamentable miseries befallen others in the like designs were easy to be found, and not forgotten to be alleged; besides their own experience, in their former troubles and hardships in their removal into Holland, and how hard a thing it was for them to live in that strange place, though it was a neighbour country and a civil and rich commonwealth.

It was answered, that all great and honourable actions are accompanied with great difficulties and must be both enterprised and overcome with answerable courages. It was granted the dangers were great, but not desperate. The difficulties were many, but not invincible. For though there were many of them likely, yet they were not certain. It might be sundry of the things feared might never befall; others by provident care and the use of good means might in a great measure be prevented; and all of them, through the help of God, by fortitude and patience, might either be borne or overcome. True it was that such attempts were not to be made and undertaken without good ground and reason, not rashly or lightly as many have done for curiosity or hope of gain, etc. But their condition was not ordinary, their ends were good and honourable, their calling lawful and urgent; and therefore they might expect the blessing of God in their proceeding. Yea, though they should lose their lives in this action, yet might they have comfort in the same and their endeavours would be honourable. They lived here but as men in exile and in a poor condition, and as great miseries might possibly befall them in this place; for the twelve years of truce were now out and there was nothing but beating of drums and preparing for war, the events whereof are always uncertain. The Spaniard might prove as cruel as the savages of America, and the famine and pestilence as sore here as there, and their liberty less to look out for remedy.

After many other particular things answered and alleged on both sides, it was fully concluded by the major part to put this design in execution and to prosecute it by the best means they could. . . .

(The Journey to America)

At length, after much travel and these debates, all things were got ready and provided. A small ship was bought and fitted in Holland, which was intended as to serve to help to transport them, so to stay in the country and attend upon fishing and such other affairs as might be for the good and benefit of the colony when they came there. Another was hired at London, of burthen about 9 score, and all other things got in readiness. So being ready to depart, they had a day of solemn humiliation, their pastor taking his text from Ezra viii. 21: "And there at the river, by Ahava, I proclaimed a fast, that we might humble ourselves before our God, and seek of him a right way for us, and for our children, and for all our substance." Upon which he spent a good part of the day very profitably and suitable to their present occasion; the rest of the time was spent in pouring out prayers to the

Lord with great fervency, mixed with abundance of tears. And the time being come that they must depart, they were accompanied with most of their brethren out of the city, unto a town sundry miles off called Deltshaven, where the ship lay ready to receive them. So they left that goodly and pleasant city which had been their resting place near twelve years; but they knew they were pilgrims, and looked not much on those things, but lift up their eyes to the heavens, their dearest country, and quieted their spirits. . . .

September 6. [1620] These troubles being blown over, and now all being compact together in one ship, they put to sea again with a prosperous wind, which continued divers days together, which was some encouragement unto them; yet, according to the usual manner, many were afflicted with seasickness. And I may not omit here a special work of God's providence. There was a proud and very profane young man, one of the seamen, of a lusty, able body, which made him the more haughty; he would alway be contemning the poor people in their sickness and cursing them daily with grievous execrations; and did not let to tell them that he hoped to help to cast half of them overboard before they came to their journey's end, and to make merry with what they had; and if he were by any gently reproved, he would curse and swear most bitterly. But it pleased God before they came half seas over, to smite this young man with a grievous disease, of which he died in a desperate manner, and so was himself the first that was thrown overboard. Thus his curses light on his own head, and it was an astonishment to all his fellows for they noted it to be the just hand of God upon him.

After they had enjoyed fair winds and weather for a season, they were encountered many times with cross winds and met with many fierce storms with which the ship was shroudly shaken, and her upper works made very leaky; and one of the main beams in the midships was bowed and cracked, which put them in some fear that the ship could not be able to perform the voyage. So some of the chief of the company, perceiving the mariners to fear the sufficiency of the ship as appeared by their mutterings, they entered into serious consultation with the master and other officers of the ship, to consider in time of the danger, and rather to return than to cast themselves into a desperate and inevitable peril. And truly there was great distraction and difference of opinion amongst the mariners themselves; fain would they do what could be done for their wages' sake (being now near half the seas over) and on the other hand they were loath to hazard their lives too desperately. But in examining of all opinions, the master and others affirmed they knew the ship to be strong and firm under water; and for the buckling of the main beam, there was a great iron screw the passengers brought out of Holland, which would raise the beam into his place; the which being done, the carpenter and master affirmed that with a post put under it, set firm in the lower deck and otherways bound, he would make it sufficient. And as for the decks and upper works, they would caulk them as well as they could, and though with the working of the ship they would not long keep staunch, yet there would otherwise be no great danger, if they did not overpress her with sails. So they committed themselves to the will of God and resolved to proceed.

In sundry of these storms the winds were so fierce and the seas so high, as they could not bear a knot of sail, but were forced to hull[4] for divers days together. And in one of them, as they thus lay at hull in a mighty storm, a lusty[5] young man called John Howland, coming upon some occasion above the gratings was, with a seele[6] of the ship, thrown into sea; but it pleased God that he caught hold of the topsail halyards which hung overboard and ran out at length. Yet he held his hold (though he was sundry fathoms under water) till he was hauled up by the same rope to the brim of the water, and then with a boat hook and other means got into the ship again and his life saved. And though he was something ill with it, yet he lived many years after and became a profitable member both in

---

[4] To heave or lay-to under very short sail and drift with the wind.

[5] Lively, merry; no sexual connotation. Howland, a servant of Governor Carver, rose to be one of the leading men of the Colony.

[6] Roll or pitch.

church and commonwealth. In all this voyage there died but one of the passengers, which was William Butten, a youth, servant to Samuel Fuller, when they drew near the coast.

But to omit other things (that I may be brief) after long beating at sea they fell with that land which is called Cape Cod; the which being made and certainly known to be it, they were not a little joyful. After some deliberation had amongst themselves and with the master of the ship, they tacked about and resolved to stand for the southward (the wind and weather being fair) to find some place about Hudson's River for their habitation. But after they had sailed that course about half the day, they fell amongst dangerous shoals and roaring breakers, and they were so far entangled therewith, as they conceived themselves in great danger; and the wind shrinking upon them withal, they resolved to bear up again for the Cape and thought themselves happy to get out of those dangers before night overtook them, as by God's good providence they did. And the next day[7] they got into the Cape Harbor[8] where they rid in safety.

A word or two by the way of this cape. It was thus first named by Captain Gosnold and his company, Anno 1602, and after by Captain Smith was called Cape James; but it retains the former name amongst seamen. Also, that point which first showed those dangerous shoals unto them they called Point Care, and Tucker's Terrour; but the French and Dutch to this day call it Malabar by reason of those perilous shoals and the losses they have suffered there.

Being thus arrived in a good harbor, and brought safe to land, they fell upon their knees and blessed the God of Heaven who had brought them over the vast and furious ocean, and delivered them from all the perils and miseries thereof, again to set their feet on the firm and stable earth, their proper element. And no marvel if they were thus joyful, seeing wise Seneca was so affected with sailing a few miles on the coast of

[7] Nov. 11/21, 1620. Thus the *Mayflower's* passage from Plymouth took 65 days.

[8] Now Provincetown Harbor.

his own Italy, as he affirmed, that he had rather remain twenty years on his way by land than pass by sea to any place in a short time, so tedious and dreadful was the same unto him.

But here I cannot but stay and make a pause, and stand half amazed at this poor people's present condition; and so I think will the reader, too, when he well considers the same. Being thus passed the vast ocean, and a sea of troubles before in their preparation (as may be remembered by that which went before), they had now no friends to welcome them nor inns to entertain or refresh their weatherbeaten bodies; no houses or much less towns to repair to, to seek for succor. It is recorded in Scripture as a mercy to the Apostle and his shipwrecked company, that the barbarians showed them no small kindness in refreshing them, but these savage barbarians, when they met with them (as after will appear) were readier to fill their sides full of arrows than otherwise. And for the season it was winter, and they that know the winters of that country know them to be sharp and violent, and subject to cruel and fierce storms, dangerous to travel to known places, much more to search an unknown coast. Besides, what could they see but a hideous and desolate wilderness, full of wild beasts and wild men—and what multitudes there might be of them they knew not. Neither could they, as it were, go up to the top of Pisgah to view from this wilderness a more goodly country to feed their hopes; for which way soever they turned their eyes (save upward to the heavens) they could have little solace or content in respect of any outward objects. For summer being done, all things stand upon them with a weatherbeaten face, and the whole country, full of woods and thickets, represented a wild and savage hue. If they looked behind them, there was the mighty ocean which they had passed and was now as a main bar and gulf to separate them from all the civil parts of the world. If it be said they had a ship to succour them, it is true; but what heard they daily from the master and company? But that with speed they should look out a place (with their shallop) where they would be, at some near distance; for the season was such as he would not stir from thence till a safe harbor was discovered by them, where they would be, and he might go without danger; and that victuals consumed apace but he must and would keep sufficient for themselves and their return. Yea, it was muttered by some that if they got not a place in time, they would turn them and their goods ashore and leave them. Let it also be considered what weak hopes of supply and succour they left behind them, that might bear up their minds in this sad condition and trials they were under; and they could not but be very small. It is true, indeed, the affections and love of their brethren at Leyden was cordial and entire towards them, but they had little power to help them or themselves; and how the case stood between them and the merchants at their coming away hath already been declared.

What could now sustain them but the Spirit of God and His grace? May not and ought not the children of these fathers rightly say: "Our fathers were Englishmen which came over this great ocean, and were ready to perish in this wilderness; but they cried unto the Lord, and He heard their voice and looked on their adversity," etc. "Let them therefore praise the Lord, because He is good: and His mercies endure forever." "Yea, let them which have been redeemed of the Lord, shew how He hath delivered them from the hand of the oppressor. When they wandered in the desert wilderness out of the way, and found no city to dwell in, both hungry and thirsty, their soul was overwhelmed in them. Let them confess before the Lord His lovingkindness and His wonderful works before the sons of men. . . .

(The Mayflower Compact, 1620)
I shall a little return back, and begin with a combination made by them before they came ashore; being the first foundation of their government in this place. Occasioned partly by the discontented and mutinous speeches that some of the strangers amongst them had let fall from them in the ship: That when they came ashore they would use their own liberty, for none had power to command them, the patent they had being for Virginia and not for New England, which belonged to another government, with which the Virginia Company had nothing to

do. And partly that such an act by them done, this their condition considered, might be as firm as any patent, and in some respects more sure.

The form was as followeth:

IN THE NAME OF GOD, AMEN.
We whose names are underwritten, the loyal subjects of our dread Sovereign Lord King James, by the Grace of God of Great Britain, France, and Ireland King, Defender of the Faith, etc.

Having undertaken, for the Glory of God and advancement of the Christian Faith and Honour of our King and Country, a Voyage to plant the First Colony in the Northern Parts of Virginia, do by these presents solemnly and mutually in the presence of God and one of another, Covenant and Combine ourselves together into a Civil Body Politic, for our better ordering and preservation and furtherance of the ends aforesaid; and by virtue hereof to enact, constitute and frame such just and equal Laws, Ordinances, Acts, Constitutions and Offices, from time to time, as shall be thought most meet and convenient for the general good of the Colony, unto which we promise all due submission and obedience. In witness whereof we have hereunder subscribed our names at Cape Cod, the 11th of November, in the year of the reign of our Sovereign Lord King James, of England, France and Ireland the eighteenth, and of Scotland the fifty-fourth. Anno Domini 1620.

After this they chose, or rather confirmed, Mr. John Carver (a man godly and well approved amongst them) their Governor for that year. And after they had provided a place for their goods, or common store (which were long in unlading for want of boats, foulness of the winter weather and sickness of divers) and begun some small cottages for their habitation; as time would admit, they met and consulted of laws and orders, both for their civil and military government as the necessity of their condition did require, still adding thereunto as urgent occasion in several times, and as cases did require.

In these hard and difficult beginnings they found some discontents and murmurings arise amongst some, and mutinous speeches and carriages in other; but they were soon quelled and overcome by the wisdom, patience, and just and equal carriage of things, by the Governor and better part, which clave faithfully together in the main.

(The Starving Time)

But that which was most sad and lamentable was, that in two or three months' time half of their company died, especially in January and February, being the depth of winter, and wanting houses and other comforts; being infected with the scurvy and other diseases which this long voyage and their inaccommodate condition had brought upon them. So as there died some times two or three of a day in the foresaid time, that of 100 and odd persons, scarce fifty remained.[9] And of these, in the time of most distress, there was but six or seven sound persons who to their great commendations, be it spoken, spared no pains night nor day, but with abundance of toil and hazard of their own health, fetched them wood, made them fires, dressed them meat, made their beds, washed their loathsome clothes, clothed and unclothed them. In a word, did all the homely and necessary offices for them which dainty and queasy stomachs cannot endure to hear named; and all this willingly and cheerfully, without any grudging in the least, showing herein their true love unto their friends and brethren; a rare example and worthy to be remembered. Two of these seven were Mr. William Brewster, their reverend Elder, and Myles Standish, their Captain and military commander, unto whom myself and many others were much beholden in our low and sick condition. And yet the Lord so upheld these persons as in this general calamity they were not at all infected either with sickness or lameness. And what I have said of these I may say of many others who

[9] Of the 102 *Mayflower* passengers who reached Cape Cod, 4 died before she made Plymouth; and by the summer of 1621 the total deaths numbered 50. Only 12 of the original 26 heads of families and 4 of the original 12 unattached men or boys were left; and of the women who reached Plymouth, all but a few died. Doubtless many of the deaths took place on board the *Mayflower* at anchor, since there was not enough shelter ashore for all; and Plymouth Harbor is so shallow that she was moored about 1½ nautical miles from the Rock.

died in this general visitation, and others yet living; that whilst they had health, yea, or any strength continuing, they were not wanting to any that had need of them. And I doubt not but their recompense is with the Lord.

But I may not here pass by another remarkable passage not to be forgotten. As this calamity fell among the passengers that were to be left here to plant, and were hasted ashore and made to drink water that the seamen might have the more beer, and one in his sickness desiring but a small can of beer, it was answered that if he were their own father he should have none. The disease began to fall amongst them also, so as almost half of their company died before they went away, and many of their officers and lustiest men, as the boatswain, gunner, three quartermasters, the cook and others. At which the Master was something strucken and sent to the sick ashore and told the Governor he should send for beer for them that had need of it, though he drunk water homeward bound.

But now amongst his company there was far another kind of carriage in this misery than amongst the passengers. For they that before had been boon companions in drinking and jollity in the time of their health and welfare, began now to desert one another in this calamity, saying they would not hazard their lives for them, they should be infected by coming to help them in their cabins; and so, after they came to lie by it, would do little or nothing for them but, "if they died, let them die." But such of the passengers as were yet aboard showed them what mercy they could, which made some of their hearts relent, as the boatswain (and some others) who was a proud young man and would often curse and scoff at the passengers. But when he grew weak, they had compassion on him and helped him; then he confessed he did not deserve it at their hands, he had abused them in word and deed. "Oh!" (saith he) "you, I now see, show your love like Christians indeed one to another, but we let one another lie and die like dogs." Another lay cursing his wife, saying if it had not been for her he had never come this unlucky voyage, and anon cursing his fellows, saying he had done this and that for some of them; he had spent so much and so much amongst them, and they were now weary of him and did not help him, having need. Another gave his companion all he had, if he died, to help him in his weakness; he went and got a little spice and made him a mess of meat once or twice. And because he died not so soon as he expected, he went amongst his fellows and swore the rogue would cozen him, he would see him choked before he made him any more meat; and yet the poor fellow died before morning. . . .

But to return. The spring now approaching, it pleased God the mortality began to cease amongst them, and the sick and lame recovered apace, which put as [it] were new life into them, though they had borne their sad affliction with much patience and contentedness as I think any people could do. But it was the Lord which upheld them, and had beforehand prepared them; many having long borne the yoke, yea from their youth. Many other smaller matters I omit, sundry of them having been already published in a journal made by one of the company, and some other passages of journeys and relations already published, to which I refer those that are willing to know them more particularly. . . .

(Wickedness Breaks Forth, 1642)

Marvelous it may be to see and consider how some kind of wickedness did grow and break forth here, in a land where the same was so much witnessed against and so narrowly looked unto, and severely punished when it was known, as in no place more, or so much, that I have known or heard of; insomuch that they have been somewhat censured even by moderate and good men for their severity in punishments. And yet all this could not suppress the breaking out of sundry notorious sins (as this year, besides other, gives us too many sad precedents and instances), especially drunkenness and uncleanness. Not only incontinency between persons unmarried, for which many both men and women have been punished sharply enough, but some married persons also. But that which is worse, even sodomy and buggery (things fearful to name) have broke forth in this land oftener than once.

I say it may justly be marveled at and cause us to fear and tremble at the consideration of our corrupt natures, which are so hardly bridled, subdued and mortified; nay, cannot by any other means but the powerful work and grace of God's Spirit. But (besides this) one reason may be that the Devil may carry a greater spite against the churches of Christ and the gospel here, by how much the more they endeavour to preserve holiness and purity amongst them and strictly punisheth the contrary when it ariseth either in church or commonwealth; that he might cast a blemish and stain upon them in the eyes of [the] world, who use to be rash in judgment. I would rather think thus, than that Satan hath more power in these heathen lands, as some have thought, than in more Christian nations, especially over God's servants in them.

Another reason may be, that it may be in this case as it is with waters when their streams are stopped or dammed up. When they get passage they flow with more violence and make more noise and disturbance than when they are suffered to run quietly in their own channels; so wickedness being here more stopped by strict laws, and the same more nearly looked unto so as it cannot run in a common road of liberty as it would and is inclined, it searches everywhere and at last breaks out where it gets vent.

A third reason may be, here (as I am verily persuaded) is not more evils in this kind, nor nothing near so many by proportion as in other places; but they are here more discovered and seen and made public by due search, inquisition and due punishment; for the churches look narrowly to their members, and the magistrates over all, more strictly than in other places. Besides, here the people are but few in comparison of other places which are full and populous and lie hid, as it were, in a wood or thicket and many horrible evils by that means are never seen nor known; whereas here they are, as it were, brought into the light and set in the plain field, or rather on a hill, made conspicuous to the view of all. . . .

(A Horrible Case of Bestiality)

And after the time of the writing of these things befell a very sad accident of the like foul nature in this government, this very year, which I shall now relate. There was a youth whose name was Thomas Granger. He was servant to an honest man of Duxbury, being about 16 or 17 years of age. (His father and mother lived at the same time at Scituate.) He was this year detected of buggery, and indicted for the same, with a mare, a cow, two goats, five sheep, two calves and a turkey. Horrible it is to mention, but the truth of the history requires it. He was first discovered by one that accidentally saw his lewd practice towards the mare. (I forbear particulars.) Being upon it examined and committed, in the end he not only confessed the fact with that beast at that time, but sundry times before and at several times with all the rest of the forenamed in his indictment. And this his free confession was not only in private to the magistrates (though at first he strived to deny it) but to sundry, both ministers and others; and afterwards, upon his indictment, to the whole Court and jury; and confirmed it at his execution. And whereas some of the sheep could not so well be known by his description of them, others with them were brought before him and he declared which were they and which were not. And accordingly he was cast by the jury and condemned, and after executed about the 8th of September, 1642. A very sad spectacle it was. For first the mare and then the cow and the rest of the lesser cattle were killed before his face, according to the law, Leviticus xx. 15; and then he himself was executed. The cattle were all cast into a great and large pit that was digged of purpose for them, and no use made of any part of them.

Upon the examination of this person and also of a former that had made some sodomitical attempts upon another, it being demanded of them how they came first to the knowledge and practice of such wickedness, the one confessed he had long used it in old England; and this youth last spoken of said he was taught it by another that had heard of such things from some in England when he was there, and they kept cattle together.

By which it appears how one wicked person may infect many, and what care all ought to have what servants they bring into their families.

But it may be demanded how came it to pass that so many wicked persons and profane people should so quickly come over into this land and mix themselves amongst them? Seeing it was religious men that began the work and they came for religion's sake? I confess this may be marveled at, at least in time to come, when the reasons thereof should not be known; and the more because here was so many hardships and wants met withal. I shall therefore endeavour to give some answer hereunto.

1. And first, according to that in the gospel, it is ever to be remembered that where the Lord begins to sow good seed, there the envious man will endeavour to sow tares.

2. Men being to come over into a wilderness, in which much labour and service was to be done about building and planting, etc., such as wanted help in that respect, when they could not have such as they would, were glad to take such as they could; and so, many untoward servants, sundry of them proved, that were thus brought over, both men and womenkind who, when their times were expired, became families of themselves, which gave increase hereunto.

3. Another and a main reason hereof was that men, finding so many godly disposed persons willing to come into these parts, some began to make a trade of it, to transport passengers and their goods, and hired ships for that end. And then, to make up their freight and advance their profit, cared not who the persons were, so they had money to pay them. And by this means the country became pestered with many unworthy persons who, being come over, crept into one place or other. . . .

(Expansion, 1644)

. . . Many having left this place (as is before noted) by reason of the straitness and barrenness of the same and their finding of better accommodations elsewhere more suitable to their ends and minds; and sundry others still upon every occasion desiring their dismissions, the church began seriously to think whether it were not better jointly to remove to some other place than to be thus weakened and as it were insensibly dissolved.[10] Many meetings and much consultation was held hereabout, and divers were men's minds and opinions. Some were still for staying together in this place, alleging men might here live if they would be content with their condition, and that it was not for want or necessity so much that they removed as for the enriching of themselves. Others were resolute upon removal and so signified that here they could not stay; but if the church did not remove, they must. Insomuch as many were swayed rather than there should be a dissolution, to condescend to a removal if a fit place could be found that might more conveniently and comfortably receive the whole, with such accession of others as might come to them for their better strength and subsistence; and some such-like cautions and limitations.

So as, with the aforesaid provisos, the greater part consented to a removal to a place called Nauset, which had been superficially viewed and the good will of the purchasers to whom it belonged obtained, with some addition thereto from the Court. But now they began to see their errour, that they had given away already the best and most commodious places to others, and now wanted themselves. For this place was about 50 miles from hence, and at an outside of the country remote from all society; also that it would prove so strait as it would not be competent to receive the whole body, much less be capable of any addition or increase; so as, at least in a short time, they should be worse there than they are now here. The which with sundry other like considerations and inconveniences made them change their reso-

[10] Bradford and likeminded Pilgrims welcomed the establishment of new towns and churches in the Colony by newcomers, as at Scituate and Taunton, but they wanted the original Plymouth church, including members of the second generation, to stick together. There was, however, a very narrow strip of arable land on Plymouth Bay; the back country was too rugged and rocky for profitable agriculture; and after the founding of Boston, ships from England found it more convenient to put in there. Boston gave them more business than Plymouth, which lay dead to windward of Cape Cod in the prevailing breezes, and where goods had to be lightered ashore instead of being landed on a wharf.

lutions. But such as were before resolved upon removal took advantage of this agreement and went on, notwithstanding; neither could the rest hinder them, they having made some beginning.

And thus was this poor church left, like an ancient mother grown old and forsaken of her children, though not in their affections yet in regard of their bodily presence and personal helpfulness; her ancient members being most of them worn away by death, and these of later time being like children translated into other families, and she like a widow left only to trust in God. Thus, she that had made many rich became herself poor. . . .

(William Bradford's Judgment, 1630)

Thus out of small beginnings greater things have been produced by His hand that made all things of nothing, and gives being to all things that are; and, as one small candle may light a thousand, so the light here kindled hath shone unto many, yea in some sort to our whole nation; let the glorious name of Jehovah have all the praise.

Suggestions for Further Reading

General Works on the Seventeenth Century

Oscar Handlin, "The Significance of the Seventeenth Century," J. M. Smith, ed., *Seventeenth-Century America* (1959)*; W. F. Craven, *The Southern Colonies in the Seventeenth Century* (1949); C. M. Andrews, *The Colonial Period in American History*, vols. 1–3 (1934–1938)*.

Virginia

Sigmund Diamond, "From Organization to Society: Virginia in the Seventeenth Century," *American Journal of Sociology*, vol. 63 (1958), pp. 457–475; Wesley F. Craven, *The Southern Colonies in the Seventeenth Century* (1949); Wesley F. Craven,

Dissolution of the Virginia Company (1932); Bernard Bailyn, "Politics and Social Structure in Virginia," J. M. Smith, ed., *Seventeenth-Century America* (1959), pp. 90–115*; Louis B. Wright, *First Gentlemen of Virginia* (1964);* Thomas J. Wertenbaker, *The Planters of Colonial Virginia* (1922).

New England

Perry Miller, *Errand into the Wilderness* (1956)*; *Orthodoxy in Massachusetts* (1933); *Nature's Nation* (1967); *The New England Mind: The Seventeenth Century* (1939)*; *The New England Mind: From Colony to Province* (1953)*; Edmund S. Morgan, *The Puritan Dilemma* (1958)*; Clinton Rossiter, *Seedtime of the Republic* (1953); Sumner C. Powell, *Puritan Village: The Formation of a New England Town* (1963)*; Edmund Morgan, *Visible Saints* (1963)*; Samuel E. Morison, *The Intellectual Life of Colonial New England* (1956)*; H. W. Schneider, *The Puritan Mind* (1930)*; *Puritanism in Seventeenth Century Massachusetts*, David D. Hall, ed. (1968)*; *The Puritans*, Perry Miller and Thomas H. Johnson, eds., 2 vols. (1938)*; Perry Miller, *Roger Williams, His Contribution to the American Tradition* (1962)*; Alan Simpson, *Puritanism in Old and New England* (1955)*; Ola E. Winslow, *Master Roger Williams* (1957)*; Emery J. Battis, *Saints and Sectaries: Anne Hutchinson and the Antinomian Controversy* (1962); Darrett Rutman, *Winthrop's Boston* (1915)*; S. E. Morison, *Builders of the Bay Colony* (1930)*; Richard S. Dunn, *Puritans and Yankees* (1962).

Other Colonies

Thomas J. Condon, *New York Beginnings: The Commercial Origins of New Netherland* (1968); S. G. Nissenson, *The Patron's Domain* (1937); M. Eugene Sirmans, *Colonial South Carolina* (1966).

Chapter Three
Roots of Expansion

*

Though the American continent contained enormous untapped wealth, hunger and disease claimed over half of Virginia's first settlers. The "starving time" took a heavy toll of human life but only briefly because people discovered in Virginia and elsewhere how to survive, and eventually how to prosper.

By the end of the colonial period most Americans enjoyed a standard of living higher than that of most Europeans. Visiting foreigners frequently noted the healthfulness and prosperity of the people. They saw few paupers and found a mass of property owning farmers, artisans, and shopkeepers whose high levels of material achievement and expectation radically altered perceptions of human possibilities.

From the beginning of time, most people had been poor. Food, clothing, and shelter were so scarce that except for a fortunate few, the masses suffered material deprivation. Nor could it be otherwise. The world's wealth was limited, and when it increased, it did so slowly; few could hope for more than subsistence. Consequently peasants and laborers, the majority of the population, fatalistically accepted the fact that their children would be peasants and laborers just as their ancestors before them had been. Some might improve their lot and even fewer live in relative comfort, but most people expected to endure along the margins of survival.

It was different in the American colonies. By the end of the colonial period, a French visitor announced that "from involuntary idleness, servile dependence, penury and useless labour," man in America had "passed to toils of a very different nature, rewarded by ample subsistence." Unlike colonists in other times and places who looked to national independence to free them from foreign exploitation, backwardness, and widespread poverty, the American colonists embarked on independence with a productive system already generating rising and substantial levels of individual welfare. When industrialization began in the nineteenth century, Americans enjoyed per capita incomes well above that of most present-day underdeveloped nations. Thus the roots of the affluence which make the elimination of poverty a realistic national goal, stretch back deep into America's colonial past. As a *society*, America has never been poor, although many Americans have known poverty.

Recruitment of Labor

Americans had to develop a new productive system in a virgin continent. They left behind European societies which, over many centuries, had slowly accumulated capital, grown in population, cleared and drained lands and brought them under cultivation, and built cities into busy commercial centers. In America, settlers found none of the factors of production except natural resources; and before they could be productively exploited, a labor force of sufficient size and quality had to be recruited.

By the end of the first fifty years of settlement, about 75,000 people lived in the colonies. On the eve of the American Revolution, their numbers had grown to over two and a half million, or ten times more than in 1700. Doubling every twenty or twenty-five years, population grew so rapidly that by the middle of the eighteenth century, the American colonies, only recently settled, had almost a third as many inhabitants as England.

Though the flood of migrants from Europe and slaves from Africa were important, they do not entirely explain why population grew at a rate higher than in England during the eighteenth century. Americans tended to marry at a younger age than Englishmen, thereby increasing a woman's period of childbearing. They married earlier because couples could easily establish and maintain independent households. England's land shortage encouraged people to limit family size and delay marriage for economic reasons. But America had land aplenty. Young couples could readily acquire farms which needed the labor of large families. Moreover, an abundant food supply sustained the health of women, particularly during the childbearing years, and kept the infant mortality rate well below England's.

Heavy immigration further accounts for the high growth rate. Fortunately for the colonies, economic dislocation and religious unrest in Europe compelled people to find a refuge across the ocean. At first most immigrants were members of persecuted and religious minorities as well as English farmers, laborers, craftsmen, and tradesmen who found it increasingly difficult to make a living. Those who came were usually neither very rich nor very poor. Lacking the means to migrate, the poorest often accepted their lot as decreed by fate; the well-to-do had too much to risk and too little to gain by migrating. But young farmers and artisans from families accustomed to owning some land or practicing a craft had unfulfilled expectations. Narrowing opportunities made it doubtful that if they remained at home they would enjoy a position comparable to that of their fathers. Economic change was squeezing the smaller landholders off the land. In the towns and cities, old crafts were declining, unable to compete with more efficient methods of industrial organization. Yeomen farmers found that rising land values priced them out of the market, making it impossible for fathers to help their children acquire land. Journeymen laboring for master craftsmen, intending someday to open shops of their own, found it harder than ever to escape from wage labor. In these circumstances, many young men decided to strike out on their own by going to America. Since many migrants were religious dissenters, who left home with groups of coreligionists and were received by brethren in America, the hardship and pain of removal and resettlement were lessened.

From the late seventeenth century to the end of the colonial period, immigrants came from increasingly diverse ethnic and religious backgrounds. Though the English predominated, substantial numbers of Scots, Scotch-Irish Presbyterians from Northern Ireland, Irish Catholics, Germans, and Dutch gave the colonies a varied ethnic composition. These groups brought with them a culture which persisted and since they often settled together, they were better able to perpetuate their traditions, though there was a good deal of intermingling and intermarriage. Instead of scattering evenly through the colonies, non-English immigrants favored particular regions, avoiding New England, flowing toward the more hospitable middle and southern colonies. Germans and Scotch-Irish particularly favored Pennsylvania with its liberal land and religious policies. In the eighteenth century, declining emigration from England, which now needed labor, led the crown to welcome immigrants from other lands to the colonies. Thus from colonial times, America's population has been ethnically diverse, the dominant English majority confident that it could absorb people from other nations.

Colonial economic development could not proceed without recruitment of an adequate labor force, and although Europe contained thousands willing to leave home, a way had to be found to organize and finance such a vast migration. Some could pay their own way across and establish themselves in America by saving money and selling property in England, and others received help from companies and proprietors in the early stages of colonization, but many had to rely on other means.

The colonies themselves possessed the resources necessary to finance recruitment. By offering grants of land (headrights) to individuals who paid another immigrant's passage to America, colonies induced ship captains, anxious over empty hulls on the return voyage to America, and farmers and planters eager to enlarge their work force, to import labor. In turn, emigrants agreed to work a number of years for a master who financed passage. Indentured servitude adapted the familiar principles of the English apprenticeship system to American needs. In England a youngster entered the service of a master in return for training, protection, and the initial capital to establish himself independently. Those who went to America and for several years entered the service of a farmer, planter, or artisan, learned a skill in the New World. During their term of service, they could own property, serve in the militia, sue in court, and at the expiration of their contract they received "freedom dues," providing them with resources to start on their own. Some became farmers, others artisans, though many died in service or later returned home.

The planter or yeoman farmer who aided the migration of indentured servants to America, thereby acquired more land, but even more important, he recruited additional workers who enabled him to expand production. The more farmers prospered, the more capital they accumulated to recruit still more labor to work more land. But indentured servants could easily run away, if mistreated or if restlessly ambitious; and when their terms of service ended, they had to be replaced by others. By these means, the colonies used land, which was abundant, to induce private capital to finance the flow of labor, which was scarce.

Not everyone came voluntarily. Economic dislocation in England increased the incidence of crime. Jobless people in motion roamed the countryside and crowded into the cities, intensifying the difficulty of maintaining law and order. The state defined many petty acts of lawbreaking as felonies but mitigated the harshness of the legal code by permitting individuals to escape imprisonment by going to America. Though many Americans objected to receiving English felons, some welcomed their cheap labor.

The Beginning of Slavery

Another important source of labor came from Africa. Unlike the indentured servants, blacks came involuntarily. Twenty Negroes arrived in Virginia in 1619, part of a Dutch ship's "cargo." Thereafter the number of blacks grew slowly. There were fewer than 3,000 in 1660 but after 1690 importations rose rapidly. By the time Americans founded a new nation on the principle that all men are created equal, a quarter million Africans labored in slavery. Comprising 20 percent of the population in 1776, slaves existed in all colonies but were especially important for the prosperity of the Southern colonies.

The origin of American Negro slavery lies shrouded in obscurity, although its tragic results are all too clear. Slavery as it existed on the eve of the Civil War did not come to America with the first cargo of Africans. Slavery was unknown in English law, and some of the Africans arriving during the first half of the seventeenth century were treated as indentured servants. In England servants often renewed their contracts repeatedly, since they could find no other employment. Though a few Negroes were freed at the end of a term of service, most were not. Eventually the gap between white and black servants widened. Because white servants came voluntarily, colonies found it wise to improve the conditions of service to attract them; but since Africans came in chains, their terms of labor did not have to be liberalized. The sharp rise in Negro population complicated the task of managing them. Informal methods of control gave way to laws, the black codes, that permanently fixed the Negro's status as chattel labor, human property with few privileges and no rights. The degraded Negroes' condition, their loss of control over their own persons, and sometimes over life itself, ruffled few feelings among white Americans who regarded blacks as inferior, a "degraded" race well suited to enslavement. At the same time, slavery's dehumanizing process cultivated racial prejudice among people who might have been inclined to regard Africans as fellow human beings and who might have reacted accordingly. Thus racism justified slavery and slavery inten-sified racism.

Slavery flourished because it was profitable for the northern merchant who imported slaves and the Southern planter who bought and employed them; profitable, that is, for everyone except the blacks. Torn from their families and homeland in Africa, Negroes were marched to the coast where ships waited to take them to the New World. Herded into cramped, filthy, stinking quarters, with hardly room to stand or lie down, man-acled one to another, poorly fed, and victims of epidemic dis-ease, Africans died in great numbers. "Their wailings were torturing beyond what words can express," confessed a slave trader. Some killed themselves rather than submit to the white man's brutality.

By the end of the colonial period labor, free and slave, white and black, spread across the coastal plain fronting the Atlantic and into the hill country further west, reaching and sometimes piercing the Appalachian Mountain chain, the first great barrier to the interior. Settlers tended to push into the valleys carved over the centuries by many rivers and streams. The valley floors had rich soils and the waterways kept settlers in touch with coastal ports, giving them access to markets and sources of supply.

The Indians

The Indians, the French, and the Spaniards were obstacles to the westward movement. In the long run, the Indians proved no match for the colonists' superior technology and more ad-vanced social organization. In the short run, however, the proc-ess of Indian removal was slow, tedious, and bloody. The colonists negotiated treaties under which tribes gave up lands in exchange for supplies. But Indians did not share the white man's conception of private property and disputes inevitably arose, especially since colonists ruthlessly cheated the red men. As whites continually encroached on hunting lands, the natives grew alarmed and fought to protect their way of life. Costly warfare erupted on each new frontier. Because the Indians were divided among numerous tribes, each independent of the other, English victory over one did not subdue the rest. Repeatedly, therefore, during a period of three centuries, Americans fought the red man until the last resistance ended in the late nineteenth century.

The Americans were ambivalent toward the Indians. They coveted their lands yet they regarded them as "noble savages," children of nature who possessed rare courage and skills for surviving in the wilderness. From them the English learned how to grow maize, or Indian corn, an important crop for survival during the early stages of settlement. At the same time the colonists regarded them as uncivilized heathen and attempted to enslave them and convert them to Christianity. The Indians resisted. Their culture was of such fragile nature, that Indians disintegrated when removed from their tribes. They thus proved unsuited to enslavement and, at best, conversion to Christianity was superficial and short-lived. "For, take a young Indian lad," wrote a French traveler, "give him the best education you possibly can, load him with your bounty, with presents, nay with riches; yet he will secretly long for his native woods . . . and on the first opportunity he can possibly find, you will see him voluntarily leave behind him all you have given him, and return with inexpressible joy to lie on the mats of his fathers."

White attitudes toward Indians were a mixture of paternalistic benevolence and fear of savagery; whichever attitude prevailed at a given time depended on whether the interests of the two groups clashed. But no comparable ambivalence existed toward the black man. Torn from their homeland, the blacks could neither resist effectively nor threaten their white masters to the extent that the Indians did. Whites found no nobility in the Negro's "savagery."

The French and Spaniards encouraged Indian resistance to block English expansion and to maintain a balance of power in the New World. Spanish control of Florida slowed development of Georgia and the Carolinas. The Indians thwarted the settlement of South Carolina backcountry until the 1760s.

The French

The French were England's chief rival. From Canada they contested for control of the Ohio Valley. Engaging in the western fur trade, erecting forts and forming alliances with Indian tribes, the French sought to confine the English to east of the Appalachians. The contest proved protracted. From time to time the competition escalated into warfare. The struggle for mastery of North America was a side show of a far greater struggle in Europe. France, under Louis XIV (1638–1715), was the most powerful nation in Europe. Britain sought to maintain a balance of power in Europe, in part, by denying France the resources and wealth of the New World.

From the end of the seventeenth century until the 1750s, England fought a series of inconclusive intercolonial wars. France and England, with their Indian allies, attacked one another's weak points, destroyed villages, impeded settlement and exchanged territory but neither side committed themselves sufficiently to achieve decisive victory. The outbreak of fresh fighting in 1754, led to "The Great War for Empire" (1754–1761). This time England, under the effective leadership of William Pitt, mobilized her wealth and power to dislodge the French from North America, thus opening the interior to American settlement. The elimination of the French and the enlargement of Britain's North American empire created new problems that eventually lead to revolution. At the time, none foresaw the consequences. For half a century the English and the Americans had coveted the west as an arena for advancing the power of the kingdom and the wealth of its subjects. The wealth of the colonies depended largely on the development of agriculture.

Colonial Agriculture

The economic development of the colonies hinged on the production of agricultural surpluses. Many farmers, however, were unable to advance beyond subsistence. Inefficient technology, labor shortages, isolation on the frontiers, difficulties in transporting goods to markets, all combined to hinder commercial agriculture. Establishing a farm was a formidable undertaking. European soils though less fertile had been tilled for generations; forests had been cleared and swamplands drained for many centuries. In America yeomen first had to clear the land of trees and shrubs, build homes and farms, and lay out roads. But they did this expectantly. Even subsistence farmers hoped eventually to produce surpluses and frontier farmers sought to make a profit by selling their homesteads to the next wave of settlers.

The farmer's entrepreneurial (or businessman's) outlook owed much to the ease with which he could acquire good land. Colonies offered settlers the abundant lands on liberal terms, usually free from the manorial obligations that oppressed the European peasantry. The New England colonies granted land to each newly created town whose original proprietors parceled out acreage to settlers. The New England system encouraged compactness of settlement since the legislatures controlled town creation. Designed to establish tightly knit communities whose members would never stray from the influence of the Puritan clergy and magistrates, this system did not survive intact in the eighteenth century, when speculators, unconstrained by religious scruples, induced colonies to grant them huge tracts of undeveloped lands far from settled communities.

Elsewhere farmers acquired lands through different means. Outside New England, acquisition was more informal. In the absence of a township system, individuals could locate wherever they pleased and hence settlement was generally less compact. In Virginia abuse of the headright system, whereby false claims enabled speculators to acquire land illegally, led the crown to sell land cheaply. The Maryland proprietors followed suit. For five shillings or one hundred pounds of tobacco, husbandmen could acquire fifty acres. Those who owed rents of a couple of shillings per acre found it easy to evade payment. Neither the crown nor the proprietors possessed efficient collection machinery and the local gentry, themselves large landowners, controlled government and connived with farmers to avoid payment.

Instead of satisfying land hunger, the availability of land intensified the desire and encouraged widespread speculation. Investments in more land than one could farm appealed to both urban and rural folk as well as to ordinary farmers and large-scale speculators. Rapid growth and shifts in population led people to expect land values to rise; a well located purchase might yield considerable profit. Virgin land appealed to farmers who wanted to abandon soil worn out by wasteful methods of farming as well as to acquire surplus acreage for later sale. Except for commerce and farming, practically no other outlets for savings or opportunities for speculation existed—no banks or insurance companies, few government securities, and no corporate stocks and bonds. Moreover, in a society where wealth defined social position and land was the principal form of wealth, the ambitious understandably sought large estates.

Yet despite the colonists' land speculations, and despite the formation in the mid-eighteenth century of large speculative land companies, those who wanted land found it easy to obtain. Large-scale speculation often proved unprofitable because absentee owners lacked resources to develop their holdings and could not afford to bear the expenses until purchasers arrived and demand developed. Though some obtained large tracts, there was too much good land available for a few to monopolize it. Yet there were exceptions. In New York's Hudson River Valley the Dutch first, and the English later, granted large manorial estates whose owners rented or leased but did not sell the land. As a result many immigrants preferred to settle elsewhere and become freeholders rather than tenants owing obligations to a manorial lord, as in Europe. Because of this Hudson River Valley situation, New York's population and economic development lagged.

Climate, soils, and markets determined the kinds of crops farmers raised. Tobacco and wheat provided the bulk of export staples, making up almost half the value of exports in 1770. Tobacco, grown largely in Virginia, Maryland, and North Carolina, was the leading export, accounting for about one quarter of the value of exports in 1770. When tobacco production began in Virginia early in the seventeenth century, the weed's potential market had hardly been tapped since it was native to the Western Hemisphere. The Spaniards acquired it from the Indians and introduced it into Europe where the habit spread. Demand grew beyond Spain's ability to supply it, offering English producers markets which they eagerly exploited. By the end of the colonial period, however, many tobacco growers found it profitable to switch to wheat because chronic overproduction of tobacco depressed prices on the world markets. During the eighteenth century wheat production rapidly rose in importance, notably in Pennsylvania, New York, and parts of Maryland and Virginia. By 1770 wheat, flour, and bread accounted for 22 percent of the value of exports to the West Indies and Europe. The swampy lands of Georgia, North Carolina, and especially South Carolina were suitable for growing rice and indigo (a textile dye) which together accounted for 14 percent of the value of colonial exports in 1770. Not all farmers, however, could raise these major staples. Less favorable soils and climate led many, particularly in New England, to produce a variety of foodstuffs for markets in the cities and the West Indies.

Farmers unable to grow the major export staples could supplement income by engaging in industries related to agriculture. Those living near uncleared forests and with access to streams cut timber, some of it for export, some for shipbuilding, urban construction, and barrel manufacture. The forests also contained animals whose furs and hides were valuable enough to support transportation costs from the trading posts to cities where consumers sported warm beaver hats.

The most important extractive industry, however, was fishing. Centered in New England, fishing became a major source of the region's income because farming was less profitable here than elsewhere. Fishing towns dotted the New England coastline affording employment for sailors and those who processed the catch. Fish accounted for 12 percent of the value of colonial exports in 1770.

Agriculture and related industries were the foundations of colonial welfare. A European agricultural revolution that had increased efficiency and expanded production, had also radically reorganized rural society. Enlightened landlords and the well-to-do farmers improved methods by consolidating holdings and pushing the less efficient off the land. With opportunities in England shrinking, many of the excluded migrated to America where abundant land enabled most men to acquire their own farms. Some farmers prospered unusually well and expanded the scale of their operations without, as in Europe, forcing others off the land. The most successful developed plantations largely in the Southern colonies, which required considerable investment of capital, employed slave labor supervised by overseers, and produced much more than was possible on family farms.

Plantations developed because larger units of production were more efficient and some farmers were able to acquire capital with which to enlarge their scale of operations. Rice growing, for instance, used a great deal of back-breaking labor. The coastal swamps of the Carolinas and Georgia had to be drained and dammed; mills had to be constructed; and all this required capital and labor beyond the means of small farmers. Tobacco, however, could easily be raised on a family farm with a slave or two. But here, also, plantations had superior advantages. Tobacco prices fluctuated violently because growers were unable to adjust supply to demand. Producers expanded production, hoping that a big crop would bring a fair return even at lower prices since distribution costs tended to be fixed. Selling more tobacco lowered a planter's fixed cost per hogshead. Moreover, those who grew tobacco on a large scale hoped to make a fortune when prices were high.

The key to expansion lay in acquisition of additional land and slaves. Farmers could enlarge their landholdings cheaply; a successful planter might obtain tens of thousands of acres, holding some of it as reserve to replace fields depleted by soil-exhausting methods of tobacco culture, and the rest as speculation for later sale. By purchasing additional slaves, the planter could clear fresh land and expand acreage under cultivation.

The planter financed expansion by plowing back profits into his operations and by borrowing. British merchants invested in American agriculture by extending credit to planters who could then expand operations and buy luxuries from England. Concentrating on tobacco, Chesapeake planters scorned commerce and urban life; dispersed settlement patterns, moreover, retarded the growth of market centers. South Carolina rice planters maintained residences on their plantations as well as in Charleston. Successful Southern merchants usually invested in plantations and became full-fledged planters. English and Scottish merchants therefore came to dominate tobacco marketing even though the bulk of the crop went to European markets after passing through British ports and paying heavy crown taxes.

In the eighteenth century, planters became chronic debtors. The planter lacked direct control over the sale of his crop, and sometimes two years passed before settlement of accounts. Without a precise idea of how much he could afford to spend on himself and on expansion, he indulged his appetite for luxuries and his ambitions to expand. Merchants encouraged these tendencies because once they had a planter in debt, he mortgaged the next year's crop and became firmly tied to the creditor. As planters raised larger crops, middlemen earned more for their marketing services. In these ways, British merchants provided credit for American expansion but at a price. In contrast, farmers, who raised crops such as wheat not marketed by English merchants, did not have access to British credit on the same scale as did Southern planters. Wheat farming, therefore, remained dominated by yeomen farmers, until the mid-eighteenth century when some planters, finding tobacco unprofitable, turned to grain farming. Planters mined the soil with one crop, often neglecting to grow enough food to feed their slaves.

The profits from agriculture, whether carried on through family farms or large plantations, financed American economic growth, made possible a relatively high average standard of living, and paid for the goods Americans purchased abroad. The production of surpluses for sale at home and abroad also stimulated commercial development in growing port cities along the

Atlantic seaboard and countless smaller towns that collected the farmer's produce and retailed foreign imports. Boston, New York, Philadelphia, Providence, and Charleston were the principal ports whose rapid growth mirrored expansion in the hinterlands they served. By the time of the American Revolution, Philadelphia, with 25,000 inhabitants, had as many people as any city in England except London.

Most American produce went to Britain, the West Indies, and southern Europe. The first important native merchant community developed in New England. Lacking staples for the English market, New Englanders financed development and imports from Britain by selling foodstuffs to West Indian sugar planters. At the outset the New Englanders acted as agents for London firms which financed the early fishing industry. Eventually, as traders accumulated capital, they gained direct control of the fishing business and the profits formerly shared with the Londoners. Americans sold their cargoes for bills of credit on London or for sugar and molasses which they profitably manufactured into rum. They thus paid for manufactures imported from England. Trading patterns were complex, because merchants roamed all over the Atlantic basin sailing from port to port seeking favorable markets, exchanging one cargo for another, and always with the object of earning credits in London.

Though Americans obtained most of their imports from Britain, they had to find markets elsewhere for many of their exports. Until 1740 they maintained a rough balance of payments for imports and exports with England sufficient to pay for manufactured goods and luxuries. During the last thirty years of the colonial period, however, the colonies chronically imported considerably more than they sold to Britain. Increasingly, they had to earn foreign exchange elsewhere, outside the British empire. These they found in the French West Indies and in southern Europe which consumed vast quantities of wheat, fish, and timber to pay for the rapid increases in American consumption of British goods.

The export of American staples led to urban growth everywhere except in the tobacco colonies. There, British and Scottish merchants (called "factors") dominated marketing because planters preferred to specialize in tobacco growing and because British traders offered easier credit than Boston or Philadelphia merchants. Moreover, the river system that penetrated the tobacco coast enabled British ships to sail to the planter's wharf thwarting the concentration of marketing activity in a few places.

Elsewhere commerce stimulated urban development in various ways. Overseas trade gave employment to those who built and serviced ships and shipping became one of the most important colonial industries. Access to raw material enabled Americans to build vessels cheaply for sale to British as well as to American merchants. The artisans, laborers, and seamen employed by the maritime industries created markets for retailers, mechanics, and nearby farmers.

Though merchants prospered and cities grew, English merchants and shippers controlled the lion's share of transatlantic trade. The American merchants were enterprising in gathering cargoes from far-flung reaches of the colonies, parlaying one cargo into another, scouring the Atlantic for profitable exchanges, but they lacked sufficient capital to displace British houses. They did, however, dominate the coastal trade.

British subjects, wherever they lived, were not free to do business and pursue profits as they saw fit. Americans were part of an empire in which an elaborate body of law regulated and constrained economic activity according to widely shared beliefs about how nations grew rich.

The Mercantilist System and American Economic Development

The emergence of the modern state which monopolized power in the hands of kings and parliaments rested in part on the ability of central authority to control revenue—the Power of the Purse. Overseas empires offered statebuilders new sources of wealth and power. Spain's emergence from obscurity to become the colossus of Europe in the sixteenth century stemmed primarily from wealth gained abroad. Spain then translated the new wealth into power in Europe. Other kingdoms followed her example.

Mercantilism was the body of assumptions which directed statesmen in pursuit of national interest. Mercantilists believed that without wealth a nation could not be secure nor could it advance its power. Gold financed armies and expansion which brought added territories with valuable resources. New sources of wealth further enlarged a nation's capacity for both war-making and expansion. Mercantilists believed that the sum of the world's wealth was fixed; a nation, therefore, could grow richer and more powerful only at the expense of another. The application of these principles varied from country to country and from time to time but governments did not hesitate to intervene directly in the economic life of the kingdom.

English mercantilism took many forms. The chartered trading companies receiving a monopoly of trade with Virginia, Bermuda, or the East Indies were typical instruments of national policy. During the first five decades of American colonization, England left the settlements fairly free to develop on their own. The end of civil war in England, the need for additional revenues, the growing importance of the colonial economies, and intensification of rivalry with the Dutch for naval supremacy led to the development of mercantilist legislation that attempted to maximize the colonies' value to the mother country.

The Navigation Acts, first adopted in 1651 and elaborated in 1662, gave British built and owned ships a monopoly of the carrying trade into which the Dutch had intruded, especially in the tobacco colonies. Certain enumerated colonial exports such as sugar, tobacco, rice, and naval stores had to be shipped directly to England for domestic consumption or reexport. The Plantation Duty (1673) attempted to prevent American merchants from evading the acts of enumeration. The Staple Act (1663) required that goods imported into the colonies from Europe come via England. Together with enumeration, this measure gave British middlemen tighter control of American trade. By funneling colonial goods through England, the crown taxed them and made the mother country the distribution center, to the advantage of British subjects *in England*. British mercantilists also sought greater self-sufficiency by providing bounties for the production of such items as naval stores and indigo which otherwise were purchased outside the empire. The mother country also encouraged the production of tropical staples consumed at home and reexported abroad through Britain by protecting colonial producers from foreign competition and giving them a monopoly of the home market.

Mercantilism was more than a system by which the mother country exploited its colonies. Conflicts among the various interests affected by British policy for the West Indies sugar islands illustrate its complexity. Sometimes two groups of colonists clashed, as did North Americans who preferred to buy sugar in the French West Indies where the terms of trade were more favorable than in the British islands, and the English sugar planters anxious to exclude the Americans from foreign sources. The sugar planters also clashed with British merchants and refiners who preferred to import the cheaper French sugar. Through political influence, the West Indies planters obtained passage of the Molasses Act (1733) placing a prohibitive duty on French sugar imported into the American colonies. For many decades, however, the law went unenforced because the northern and middle colonies relied on illegal trade with the French islands to finance English imports, a trade which Britain permitted. The necessity to evade the Molasses Act arose because colonies not producing staples had to find markets outside the empire.

Increasingly in the eighteenth century, Britain valued the colonies not only for their raw materials but as markets for industrial products. The growth of industry in Britain made the protected American market one of the foundations of national prosperity. With a large and growing population of freehold farmers who could afford English goods, the American colonies became England's most important overseas customer, outdistancing the West Indies in the late colonial period. Thus as Britain was industralized, the colonies—which had failed to conform to the mercantilist ideal as producers of staples desired in the mother country—became valuable as customers for the industry of the mother country.

The growing importance of colonial markets led to British restrictions on the development of colonial industry. The Woolen Act (1699), the Hat Act (1732), and the Iron Act (1750) sought to discourage manufacturing. Iron production, for instance, grew rapidly in the eighteenth century, the Americans producing a seventh of the world's iron supply, manufacturing it into nails and axes, pots and pans, that otherwise would have come from England. The Iron Act encouraged colonial production of pig iron but discouraged fabrication into finished goods, hoping thereby to lessen the dependence of English manufacturers on foreign sources but assuring them a monopoly of the American market for finished iron goods.

The crown also regulated colonial efforts to provide an adequate supply of currency and credit. There were no banks in the colonies nor did Britain provide Americans with an adequate money supply, but when colonists resorted to local expedients they faced British disapproval and prohibition. Until the 1750s they managed to evade English restraints designed to protect British merchants from receiving in payment of debts cheap colonial paper money, though the paper money was often a stable medium strongly favored by American merchants.

The mercantilist system, like any other, had advantages and disadvantages. The navigation acts benefited colonial shipbuilding and shipping interests, eliminating foreign competition, and bounties subsidized certain producers. Though the colonists were not free to import goods from outside the empire, England as the most advanced industrial nation could undersell foreign competition and cater to colonial tastes; even after independence, the Americans continued to buy English manufactures. Enumeration favored British merchants and raised the distribution costs of staples which had to pass through England on their way to the Continent. But English merchants provided valuable services, developed foreign markets, and extended credits to planters whose exports enjoyed preferential treatment in the English market. Though American merchants had to accept a makeshift supply of currency and credit, they had access to English capital, enjoyed the protection of the British navy and, in wartime, government contracts made many American fortunes. Where mercantilism most pinched, as in the West Indies sugar trade, lax enforcement opened loopholes through which Americans scrambled.

Restraints on American industrial development were premature. The preconditions for industry did not exist in the colonies nor did they appear until forty years after independence. Labor and capital, in short supply, flowed into agriculture, and the domestic market for factory products was limited by the thinly distributed population, poorly linked by inefficient means of communication. Americans possessed limited purchasing power to support their own industries. A high degree of self-sufficiency limited the market for manufactures. Crude technology and high transportation costs moreover constricted industrial possibilities. In contrast, British manufacturers had large domestic markets, supplemented by additional outlets throughout the world.

British mercantilists regarded the colonies as a means of advancing the wealth and power of the kingdom. Britain prospered from its overseas dependencies but so too did the colonists who flourished economically despite the mother country's restrictions. By 1776 Americans were materially prepared for independence. A century long policy of British regulation aimed at keeping them subordinate had failed.

The Prosperous Americans

American welfare rested on the productivity of its farms and plantations. Surpluses collected by merchants enabled farmers to buy things produced elsewhere. The natural resources of a rich unexploited continent provided the foundation of American economic development. An enterprising people, able to acquire land easily and accumulate or borrow capital, produced commodities that found eager buyers in world markets. By the time Americans separated from England, they had developed an agricultural system—owned and operated by colonials rather than by absentee proprietors in Britain—and an indigenous and experienced urban business community. In the formative years of American settlement, the necessity to recruit laborers from England and the willingness of the colonies to attract people by offering them land created a numerous body of freehold farmers, except in parts of the Southern colonies.

Though England profited extensively from its North American provinces, much wealth remained in the hands of colonists who produced it. Colonies in other times and places fared less well. In Africa and Asia, Europeans enslaved and exploited native populations, foreigners owned and managed most enterprises, enjoying the profits and determining the course of economic development. The Americans were more fortunate. Settling a continent populated sparsely by Indians, the British developed their North American colonies by attracting free labor and offering wide scope for the enterprise of diverse individuals and many groups. At the same time that opportunities in farming were diminishing in England, as a limited supply of land became increasingly concentrated in the hands of a few, America was becoming a land of independent yeomen whose numbers rapidly multiplied. Colonial prosperity, moreover, was less vulnerable to sharp fluctuations in the marketplace than was the case in the nineteenth century when the disappearance of subsistence farming and home manufacturing gave way to the growth of specialization of production for foreign and domestic markets. Regional interdependence and specialization then locked citizens in the grip of the business cycle, with its alternating periods of boom and depression.

During the 175 years of the colonial period, people discovered that the mass of men, at least in America, need not be poor. Natural resources were so abundant that, if appropriately distributed, most whites could be decently fed, clothed, and sheltered. Shrewd and hard-working individuals could improve their lot in life and their children might realistically entertain aspirations for social advancement that few sons of farmers and artisans in Europe could expect. This revolution of rising material and social expectations inevitably affected the forms of government under which Americans lived.

Document: The African Slave Trade
The Voyage of the <u>Hannibal</u>, 1693–1694

The following is an account of the African slave trade from the Journal of Thomas Phillips, commander of the ship <u>Hannibal</u>, *1693–1694. Members of the Royal African Company to whom Britain granted a monopoly of the slave trade maintained "factories," that is, business headquarters, on the Slave Coast in Africa where they purchased slaves from local chiefs and dealers. The* <u>Hannibal's</u> *cargo was destined for the West Indies where slaves were employed on plantations and seasoned for sale in the North American colonies. Phillips' attitude toward blacks was ambivalent. He condemned as barbaric the practice of some slavers who cut off the legs of troublesome captives to terrify the rest. Negroes, he believed, were as much the children of God as whites and were not racially inferior. Yet he expressed no qualms about enslaving them and engaging in a business that took a high death toll of the Africans. So brutalizing was the slave trade to black and white alike that in the end Phillips regarded his cargo as "a parcel of creatures nastier than swine" though he had earlier described them as "the works of God's hands, and no doubt as dear to him as ourselves."*

May the 21st. This morning I went ashore at Whidaw, accompany'd by my doctor and purser, Mr. Clay, the present Capt. of the *East-India Merchant,* his doctor and purser, and about a dozen of our seamen for our guard, arm'd, in order here to reside till we could purchase 1300 negro slaves, which was the number

Source: Elizabeth Donnan, ed., *Documents Illustrating the History of the Slave Trade to America* (4 vols., 1930–1935), I, pp. 399–403, 406–410.

we both wanted, to compleat 700 for the *Hannibal*, and 650 for the *East-India Merchant*, according to our agreement in our charter-parties with the royal African company; in procuring which quantity of slaves we spent about nine weeks. . . .

Our factory [at Whydah] lies about three miles from the sea-side, where we were carry'd in hamocks, which the factor Mr. Joseph Peirson, sent to attend our landing, with several arm'd blacks that belong'd to him for our guard; we were soon truss'd in a bag, toss'd upon negroes heads, and convey'd to our factory. . . .

Our factory built by Capt. Wilburne, Sir John Wilburne's brother, stands low near the marshes, which renders it a very unhealthy place to live in; the white men the African company send there, seldom returning to tell their tale: 'tis compass'd round with a mud-wall, about six foot high, and on the south-side is the gate; within is a large yard, a mud thatch'd house, where the factor lives, with the white men; also a store-house, a trunk for slaves, and a place where they bury their dead white men, call'd, very improperly, the hog-yard; there is also a good forge, and some other small houses. . . . And here I must observe that the rainy season begins about the middle of May, and ends the beginning of August, in which space it was my misfortune to be there, which created sicknesses among my negroes aboard, it being noted for the most malignant season by the blacks themselves, who while the rain lasts will hardly be prevail'd upon to stir out of their huts. . . .

The factory prov'd beneficial to us in another kind; for after we had procured a parcel of slaves, and sent them down to the sea-side to be carry'd off, it sometimes proved bad weather, and so great a sea, that the canoes could not come ashore to fetch them, so that they returned to the factory, where they were secured and provided for till good weather presented, and then were near to embrace the opportunity, we sometimes shipping off a hundred of both sexes at a time.

The factor, Mr. Peirson, was a brisk man, and had good interest with the king, and credit with the subjects, who knowing their tempers, which is very dastard, had good skill in treating them both civil and rough, as occasion requir'd; most of his slaves belonging to the factory, being gold coast negroes, who are very bold, brave, and sensible, ten of which would beat the best forty men the king of Whidaw had in his kingdom; besides their true love, respect and fidelity to their master, for whose interest or person they will most freely expose their own lives. . . .

As soon as the king understood of our landing, he sent two of his cappasheirs, or noblemen, to compliment us at our factory, where we design'd to continue, that night, and pay our devoirs to his majesty next day, which we signify'd to them, and they, by a foot-express, to their monarch; whereupon he sent two more of his grandees to invite us there that night, saying he waited for us, and that all former captains used to attend him the first night: whereupon being unwilling to infringe the custom, or give his majesty any offence, we took our hamocks, and Mr. Peirson, myself, Capt. Clay, our surgeons, pursers, and about 12 men, arm'd for our guard, were carry'd to the king's town, which contains about 50 houses. . . .

We returned him thanks by his interpreter, and assur'd him how great affection our masters, the royal African company of England, bore to him, for his civility and fair and just dealings with their captains; and that notwithstanding there were many other places, more plenty of negro slaves that begg'd their custom, yet they had rejected all the advantageous offers made them out of their good will to him, and therefore had sent us to trade with him, to supply his country with necessaries, and that we hop'd he would endeavour to continue their favour by his kind usage and fair dealing with us in our trade, that we may have our slaves with all expedition, which was the making of our voyage; that he would oblige his cappasheirs to do us justice, and not impose upon us in their prices; all of which we should faithfully relate to our masters, the royal African company, when we came to England. He answer'd that the African company was a very good brave man; that he lov'd him; that we should be fairly dealt with, and not impos'd upon; But he did not prove as good as his word; nor indeed (tho' his cappasheirs shew him so much respect) dare he do any thing but what they please . . . so after having examin'd us about our cargoe, what sort of goods we had, and what quantity of slaves we wanted, etc., we took our leaves and return'd to the factory, having promised to come in the morning to make our palavera, or agreement, with him about prices, how much of each of our goods for a slave.

According to promise we attended his majesty with samples of our goods, and made our agreement about the prices, tho' not without much difficulty; he and his cappasheirs exacted very high, but at length we concluded as per the latter end; then we had warehouses, a kitchen, and lodgings assign'd us, but none of our rooms had doors till we made them, and put on locks and keys; next day we paid our customs to the king and cappasheirs, as will appear hereafter; then the bell was order'd to go about to give notice to all people to bring their slaves to the trunk to sell us: this bell is a hollow piece of iron in shape of a sugar loaf, the cavity of which could contain about 50 lb. of cowries: This a man carry'd about and beat with a stick, which made a small dead sound. . . .

Capt. Clay and I had agreed to go to the trunk to buy the slaves by turns, each his day, that we might have no distraction or disagreement in our trade, as often happens when there are here more ships than one, and the commanders can't set their horses together, and go hand in hand in their traffick, whereby they have a check upon the blacks, whereas their disagreements create animosities, underminings, and out-bidding each other, whereby they enhance the prices to their general loss and detriment, the blacks well knowing how to make the best use of such opportunities, and as we found make it their business, and endeavour to create and foment misunderstandings and jealousies between commanders, it turning to their great account in the disposal of their slaves.

When we were at the trunk, the king's slaves, if he had any, were the first offer'd to sale, which the cappasheirs would be very urgent with us to buy, and would in a manner force us to it ere they would shew us any other, saying they were the

Reys Cosa, and we must not refuse them, tho' as I observ'd they were generally the worst slaves in the trunk, and we paid more for them than any others, which we could not remedy, it being one of his majesty's prerogatives: then the cappasheirs each brought out his slaves according to his degree and quality, the greatest first, etc. and our surgeon examin'd them well in all kinds, to see that they were sound wind and limb, making them jump, stretch out their arms swiftly, looking in their mouths to judge of their age; for the cappasheirs are so cunning, that they shave them all close before we see them, so that let them be never so old we can see no grey hairs in their heads or beards; and then having liquor'd them well and sleek with palm oil, 'tis no easy matter to know an old one from a middle-age one, but by the teeths decay; but our greatest care of all is to buy none that are pox'd, lest they should infect the rest aboard. . . .

When we had selected from the rest such as we liked, we agreed in what goods to pay for them, the prices being already stated before the king, how much of each sort of merchandize we were to give for a man, woman, and child, which gave us much ease, and saved abundance of disputes and wranglings, and gave the owner a note, signifying our agreement of the sorts of goods; upon delivery of which the next day he receiv'd them; then we mark'd the slaves we had bought in the breast, or shoulder, with a hot iron, having the letter of the ship's name on it, the place being before anointed with a little palm oil, which caus'd but little pain, the mark being usually well in four or five days, appearing very plain and white after.

When we had purchas'd to the number of 50 or 60 we would send them aboard, there being a cappasheir, intitled the captain of the slaves, whose care it was to secure them to the water-side, and see them all off; and if in carrying to the marine any were lost, he was bound to make them good, to us, the captain of the trunk being oblig'd to do the like, if any ran away while under his care, for after we buy them we give him charge of them till the captain of the slaves comes to carry them away: These are two officers appointed by the king for this purpose, to each of which every ship pays the value of a slave in what goods they like best for their trouble, when they have done trading; and indeed they discharg'd their duty to us very faithfully, we not having lost one slave thro' their neglect in 1300 we bought here.

There is likewise a captain of the sand, who is appointed to take care of the merchandize we have come ashore to trade with, that the negroes do not plunder them, we being often forced to leave goods a whole night on the sea shore, for want of porters to bring them up; but notwithstanding his care and authority, we often came by the loss, and could have no redress.

When our slaves were come to the seaside, our canoes were ready to carry them off to the longboat, if the sea permitted, and she convey'd them aboard ship, where the men were all put in irons, two and two shackled together, to prevent their mutiny, or swimming ashore.

The negroes are so wilful and loth to leave their own country, that they have often leap'd out of the canoes, boat and ship, into the sea, and kept under water till they were drowned, to avoid being taken up and saved by our boats, which pursued them; they having a more dreadful apprehension of Barbadoes than we can have of hell, tho' in reality they live much better there than in their own country; but home is home, etc: we have likewise seen divers of them eaten by the sharks, of which a prodigious number kept about the ships in this place, and I have been told will follow her hence to Barbadoes, for the dead negroes that are thrown over-board in the passage. I am certain in our voyage there we did not want the sight of some every day, but that they were the same I can't affirm.

We had about 12 negroes did wilfully drown themselves, and others starv'd themselves to death; for 'tis their belief that when they die they return home to their own country and friends again.

I have been inform'd that some commanders have cut off the legs and arms of the most wilful, to terrify the rest, for they believe if they lose a member, they cannot return home again: I was advis'd by some of my officers to do the same, but I could not be perswaded to entertain the least thought of it, much less put in practice such barbarity and cruelty to poor creatures, who, excepting their want of christianity and true religion (their misfortune more than fault) are as much the works of God's hands, and no doubt as dear to him as ourselves; nor can I imagine why they should be despis'd for their colour, being what they cannot help, and the effect of the climate it has pleas'd God to appoint them. I can't think there is any intrinsick value in one colour more than another, nor that white is better than black, only we think so because we are so, and are prone to judge favourably in our own case, as well as the blacks, who in odium of the colour, say, the devil is white, and so paint him. . . .

The present king often, when ships are in a great strait for slaves, and cannot be supply'd otherwise, will sell 3 or 400 of his wives to compleat their number, but we always pay dearer for his slaves than those bought of the cappasheirs, his measure for booges being much larger than theirs, and he was allow'd accordingly in all other goods we had.

For every slave the cappasheirs sold us publickly, they were oblig'd to pay part of the goods they receiv'd for it to the king, as toll or custom, especially the booges, of which he would take a small dishfull out of each measure; to avoid this they would privately send for us to their houses in the night, and dispose of two or three slaves at a time, and we as privately would send them the goods agreed upon for them; but this they did not much practise for fear of offending the king, should he come to know it, who enjoyns them to carry all their slaves to be sold publickly at the trunk with his own; sometimes after he had sold one of his wives or subjects, he would relent, and desire us to exchange for another, which we freely did often, and he took very kindly. . . .

. . . When our slaves are aboard we shackle the men two and two, while we lie in port, and in sight of their own country, for 'tis then they attempt to make their escape, and mutiny; to prevent which we always keep centinels upon the hatchways, and have a chest full of small arms, ready loaden and prim'd, constantly lying at hand upon the quarter-deck, together with some granada shells; and two of our quarter-deck guns, pointing on the deck thence, and two more out of the steerage, the door of which is always kept shut, and well barr'd; they are fed twice a day, at 10 in the morning, and 4 in the evening, which is the time they are aptest to mutiny, being all upon deck; therefore all that time, what of our men are not employ'd in distributing their victuals to them, and settling them, stand to their arms; and some with lighted matches at the great guns that yaun upon them, loaden with partridge, till they have done and gone down to their kennels between decks: Their chief diet is call'd dabbadabb, being Indian corn ground as small as oat-meal, in iron mills, which we carry for that purpose; and after mix'd with water, and boil'd well in a large copper furnace, till 'tis as thick as a pudding, about a peckful of which in vessels, call'd crews, is allow'd to 10 men, with a little salt, malagetta, and palm oil, to relish; they are divided into messes of ten each, for the easier and better order in serving them: Three days a week they have horse-beans boil'd for their dinner and supper, great quantities of which the African company do send aboard us for that purpose; these beans the negroes extremely love and desire, beating their breast, eating them, and crying Pram! Pram! which is Very good! they are indeed the best diet for them, having a binding quality, and consequently good to prevent the flux, which is the inveterate distemper that most affects them, and ruins our voyages by their mortality: The men are all fed upon the main deck and forecastle, that we may have them all under command of our arms from the quarterdeck, in case of any disturbance; the women eat upon the quarterdeck with us, and the boys and girls upon the poop; after they are once divided into messes, and appointed their places, they will readily run there in good order of themselves afterwards; when they have eaten their victuals clean up, (which we force them to for to thrive the better) they are order'd down between decks, and every one as he passes has a pint of water to drink after his meal, which is serv'd them by the cooper out of a large tub, fill'd before-hand ready for them. . . .

When we come to sea we let them all out of irons, they never attempting then to rebel, considering that should they kill or master us, they could not tell how to manage the ship, or must trust us, who would carry them where we pleas'd; therefore the only danger is while we are in sight of their own country, which they are loth to part with; but once out of sight out of mind: I never heard that they mutiny'd in any ships of consequence, that had a good number of men, and the least care; but in small tools where they had but few men, and those negligent or drunk, then they surpriz'd and butcher'd them, cut the cables, and let the vessel drive ashore, and every one shift for himself. However, we have some 30 or 40 gold coast negroes, which we buy, and are procur'd us there by our factors, to make guardians and overseers of the Whidaw negroes, and sleep among them to keep them from quarrelling; and in order, as well as to give us notice, if they can discover any caballing or plotting among them, which trust they will discharge with great diligence: they also take care to make the negroes scrape the decks where they lodge every morning very clean, to eschew any distempers that may engender from filth and nastiness; when we constitute a guardian, we give him a cat of nine tails as a badge of his office, which he is not a little proud of, and will exercise with great authority. We often at sea in the evenings would let the slaves come up into the sun to air themselves, and make them jump and dance for an hour or two to our bag-pipes, harp, and fiddle, by which exercise to preserve them in health; but notwithstanding all our endeavour, 'twas my hard fortune to have great sickness and mortality among them.

Having bought my compliment of 700 slaves, *viz.* 480 men and 220 women, and finish'd all my business at Whidaw, I took my leave of the old king, and his cappasheirs, and parted, with many affectionate expressions on both sides, being forced to promise him that I would return again the next year, with several things he desired me to bring him from England; and having sign'd bills of lading to Mr. Peirson, for the negroes aboard, I set sail the 27th of July in the morning, accompany'd with the *East-India Merchant*, who had bought 650 slaves, for the island of St. Thomas, with the wind at W.S.W. . . . .

Having completed all my business ashore in fourteen days that I lay here, yesterday in the afternoon I came off with a resolution to go to sea. Accordingly about six in the evening we got up our anchors, and set sail for Barbadoes, being forc'd to leave the *East-India merchant* behind, who could not get ready to sail in nine or ten days; which time I could not afford to stay, in respect to the mortality of my negroes, of which two or three died every day, also the small quantity of provisions I had to serve for my passage to Barbadoes. . . .

We spent in our passage from St. Thomas to Barbadoes two months eleven days, from the 25th of August to the 4th of November following: in which time there happen'd much sickness and mortality among my poor men and negroes, that of the first we buried 14, and of the last 320, which was a great detriment to our voyage, the royal African company losing ten pounds by every slave that died, and the owners of the ship ten pounds ten shillings, being the freight agreed on to be paid them by the charter-party for every negroe deliver'd alive ashore to the African company's agents at Barbadoes; whereby the loss in all amounted to near 6560 pounds sterling. The distemper which my men as well as the blacks mostly die of, was the white flux, which was so violent and inveterate, that no medicine would in the least check it; so that when any of our men were seiz'd with it, we esteem'd him a dead man, as he generally proved. I cannot imagine what should cause it in them so suddenly, they being free from it till about a week after we left the island of St. Thomas. And next to the malignity of the climate, I can attribute it to nothing else but the unpurg'd black sugar, and raw unwholesome rum they bought there, of which they drank in punch to great excess, and which it was not in my power to hinder, having chastis'd several of them, and flung over-board what rum and sugar I could find. . . .

The negroes are so incident to the small-pox, that few ships that carry them escape without it, and sometimes it makes vast havock and destruction among them: but tho' we had 100 at a time sick of it, and that it went thro' the ship, yet we lost not above a dozen by it. All the assistance we gave the diseased was only as much water as they desir'd to drink, and some palm-oil to anoint their sores, and they would generally recover without any other helps but what kind nature gave them.

One thing is very surprizing in this distemper among the blacks, that tho' it immediately infects those of their own colour, yet it will never seize a white man; for I had several white men and boys aboard that had never had that distemper, and were constantly among the blacks that were sick of it, yet none of them in the least catch'd it, tho' it be the very same malady in its effects, as well as symptoms, among the blacks, as among us in England, beginning with the pain in the head, back, shivering, vomiting, fever, etc. But what the small-pox spar'd, the flux swept off, to our great regret, after all our pains and care to give them their messes in due order and season, keeping their lodgings as clean and sweet as possible, and enduring so much misery and stench so long among a parcel of creatures nastier than swine; and after all our expectations to be defeated by their mortality. No gold-finders can endure so much noisome slavery as they do who carry negroes; for those have some respite and satisfaction, but we endure twice the misery; and yet by their mortality our voyages are ruin'd, and we pine and fret our selves to death, to think that we should undergo so much misery, and take so much pains to so little purpose.

I deliver'd alive at Barbadoes to the company's factors 372, which being sold, came out at about nineteen pounds per head one with another. . . .

Suggestions for Further Reading

Colonial Economic Development

Stuart Bruchey, *Roots of American Economic Growth,* 1607–1861 (1965), chaps. 2, 3*; George R. Taylor, "American

Economic Growth before 1840," *Journal of Economic History*, vol. 24 (1964), pp. 427–444.

Westward Movement

Ray Billington, *Westward Expansion* (1949). Verner W. Crane, *Southern Frontier: 1670–1732* (1928).*

Immigration and Labor

Mildred Campbell, *The English Yeoman under Elizabeth and Early Stuarts* (1942); "Social Origins of Some Early Americans," J. M. Smith ed., *Seventeenth-Century America* (1959), pp. 63–89*; Abbott E. Smith, *Colonists in Bondage* (1947); Richard B. Morris, *Government and Labor in Early America* (1946)*; Marcus Lee Hansen, *The Atlantic Migration* (1940)*; Oscar Handlin, *The Uprooted* (1951)*; Ian C. Graham, *Colonists from Scotland* (1956); Carl Bridenbaugh, *The Colonial Craftsman* (1950).*

Slavery

Oscar and Mary F. Handlin, *Race and Nationality in American Life* (1957), chap. 1*; Carl Degler, "Slavery and the Genesis of American Race Prejudice," *Comparative Studies in Society and History*, vol. 2 (1959), pp. 49–66, 488–495; David B. Davis, *The Problem of Slavery in Western Culture* (1966)*; Stanley Elkins, *Slavery: A Problem in American Institutional and Intellectual Life* (1959)*; Winthrop D. Jordan, *White over Black* (1968)*; Kenneth Stampp, *The Peculiar Institution* (1956)*; J. H. Franklin, *From Slavery to Freedom* (1947)*; *The Indian and the White Man*, Wilcomb E. Washburn, ed., (1964)*; Alden T. Vaughan, *New England Frontier, Puritans and Indians, 1620–1675* (1965)*; Roy H. Pearce, *The Savages of America* (1953)*; Allen Trelease, *Indian Affairs in Colonial New York* (1960).

The Struggle for North America

Howard H. Peckham, *The Colonial Wars: 1689–1762* (1964); Max Savelle, *Origins of American Diplomacy* (1967);

Walter L. Dorn, *Competition for Empire* (1940)*; Stanley M. Pargellis, *Lord Loudoun in North America* (1933); Robert C. Newbold, *The Albany Congress and Plan of Union of 1754* (1955); Lawrence H. Gipson, *British Empire before the American Revolution*, vol. 5 (1942); John Shy, *Toward Lexington* (1966), chap. 1.*

Colonial Agriculture

L. C. Gray, *History of Agriculture in the Southern United States to 1860* (1933), vol. 1; Jacob Price, "The Economic Growth of the Chesapeake and the European Market, 1695–1775," *Journal of Economic History*, vol. 25 (1964), pp. 496–511; Aubrey C. Land, "Economic Behavior in a Planting Society: The Eighteenth-Century Chesapeake," *Journal of Southern History*, vol. 33 (1967), pp. 469–485.

Land System

Roy H. Akagi, *Town Proprietors of New England* (1924); Shaw Livermore, *Early American Land Companies* (1939); Roy F. Robbins, *Our Landed Heritage* (1942)*; Marshall Harris, *Origin of the Land Tenure System in the United States* (1953).

Currency

Curtis P. Nettels, *Money Supply of American Colonies before 1720* (1934); E. James Ferguson, *The Power of the Purse* (1961); chap. 1*; Bray Hammond, *Banks and Politics in America* (1957), chap. 1*.

Mercantilism

Jacob Viner, "Power versus Plenty as Objectives of Foreign Policy in the Seventeenth and Eighteenth Centuries," *World Politics*, vol. 1 (1948), pp. 1–29; Lawrence A. Harper, *The English Navigation Laws* (1939); Oliver M. Dickerson, *Navigation Acts and the American Revolution* (1951)*; George L. Beer, *The Origins of the British Colonial System 1578–1660* (1908); G. L. Beer, *The Old Colonial System 1660–1668* (1912); Robert P. Thomas, "A Quantitative Approach to the Study of the Effects of British Imperial Policy upon Colonial Welfare," *Journal of Economic History*, vol. 25 (1965), pp. 615–638; Viola F. Barnes, *The Dominion of New England* (1933); Richard B. Sheridan, "The Molasses Act and the Market Strategy of the British Sugar Planters," *Journal of Economic History*, vol. 18 (1957), pp. 62–83; Charles M. Andrews, *The Colonial Period in American History: England's Commercial and Colonial Policy*, vol. 4 (1938)*; Curtis P. Nettels, "British Mercantilism and the Economic Development of the Thirteen Colonies," *Journal of Economic History*, vol. 12 (Spring, 1952).

Colonial Commerce

Bernard Bailyn, *The New England Merchants in the Seventeenth Century* (1955)*; Stuart Bruchey ed., *The Colonial Merchant* (1967)*; W. T. Baxter, *The House of Hancock* (1945); James B. Hedges, *The Browns of Providence Plantations* (1952); Richard Pares, *Yankees and Creoles: The Trade between North America and the West Indies before the American Revolution* (1956); Richard Pares, *Merchants and Planters* (1960); Leila Sellers, *Charleston Business on the Eve of the Revolution* (1934).

Colonial Cities

Carl Bridenbaugh, *Cities in the Wilderness* (1938); Carl Bridenbaugh, *Cities in Revolt* (1955)*; Carl and Jessica Bridenbaugh, *Rebels and Gentlemen: Philadelphia in the Age of Franklin* (1942)*; Sam B. Warner, Jr., *The Private City, Philadelphia in Three Periods of Its Growth* (1968) chaps. 1–2; Charles N. Glaab and A. Theodore Brown, *A History of Urban America* (1967), chap. 1*.

Chapter Four

From Plantations to Commonwealths

Democratic government, unknown in Europe since the collapse of ancient Greek democracy, was rediscovered in the New World. Colonists brought political ideas and practices from Europe where kings and aristocrats monopolized political power. They did not intend to innovate, yet during the colonial period Americans achieved a large degree of self-government and managed their own affairs in ways that pointed toward popular rule. Though colonists did not know full-scale democracy nor did they possess the political parties through which modern democracies govern themselves, they were laying the foundations for both. In the half century following independence, Americans completed the transformations in government begun during the colonial period.

Throughout the colonial period, Europeans shared common assumptions about the uses of power. Governments existed to establish order among men whose passions, if left unchecked, would create chaos or anarchy. By protecting the peace, establishing and upholding a rule of law to guide individual behavior, the state made civilized existence possible. The responsibilities of wielding power fell to that small element in society fit to rule. The mass of men were no more capable of governing themselves

103

than of existing without government. Power was the privilege of the wealthy, educated, and intelligent elite. Peasants, artisans, and laborers should work at their occupations, jobs which they could perform well, and leave decision-making to their superiors. In this way the various elements in society performed those functions for which each was best suited.

The politically responsible strata were thus identical with the social elite; power flowed down from the top of the social structure, from the king and the great nobility and lesser aristocracy down to the merchants, shopkeepers, farmers, and laborers subject to their authority. Furthermore, by the seventeenth century, the new nation-states lodged ultimate power in some central institution, the monarchy, or the monarchy and Parliament, as the best way of maintaining order and promoting the country's interests.

Though a few governed, they were not at liberty to tyrannize. In theory, the king and nobility must promote the well-being of all. They were no more free to do as they pleased than those they governed. Theoretically, the welfare of society mattered more than the claims of individuals, high or low in the social structure, and the state could rigorously discipline dissidents if necessary. Government gained its legitimacy from still another source, especially in England where a long medieval tradition established the principle that rulers must govern in accordance with their responsibilities as Christians and within limits established by their subjects through custom and law. Parliament became the principal instrument through which representative government developed in England.

By the end of the colonial period Americans had transformed traditional political ideas and arrangements. The need for order in a wilderness society was at least as great as in the Old World. But Americans managed their public affairs differently. Legally, power in the empire flowed from the top down, since supreme authority centered in the crown and Parliament which made and administered the laws governing the colonies.

But from the beginning, power in America drained away into the local units of governments—the towns, the counties, and the provincial legislatures—and power flowed from the bottom up as well as from England to America. Compared to those who ruled in England, native American leadership came from socially inferior classes, often men who had risen from obscurity to positions of wealth and power. The American governing classes also had to pay much more attention to the interests and wishes of those they governed than their counterparts in England. Whereas the great majority of adult males could not participate in English politics, in the colonies generally a majority of adult white males could vote in local and provincial elections, though many did not exercise this privilege.

In America rulers found it increasingly difficult to impose a conception of the general welfare that constrained the various groups and interests. By the end of the colonial period, colonists were far more likely to question and even oppose authority than was the case in England, as a bewildering variety of elements competed for advantage. Increasingly, people came to view the state as the individual's servant, not his master. Government, many believed, must allow citizens to pursue their interests even at the expense of the welfare of others, though few explicitly repudiated the community's right to limit individual freedom for the common good. In America, however, it was harder for men to agree on what *was* the common good, and still harder for any one group to make others accept its particular version.

The Beginnings of Government

Three thousand miles away from the courts, the king, and the Parliament that had governed them at home, settlers had to frame laws and establish governments in a wilderness. Disorder threatened civilized existence in the New World as it did in the Old. Political authority had to develop in the colonies without central direction or plan. Since the crown delegated colonization to private enterprise, it removed itself in the beginning from direct responsibility for governing. Internal conflict within England between Puritans and Anglicans, and king and Parliament until 1660 left the colonizing groups free to proceed as they wished. Yet despite the absence of central control or uniformity in the methods of settlement, political development followed a common pattern.

At first, the founders of each settlement—whether the Puritan elite in Massachusetts, the officers of the Virginia Company, or the proprietor of Maryland—attempted to concentrate power in their own hands. In every case events thwarted their plans. None had the power to impose his will on the settlers for long; prudence and necessity led to a dispersal of power. The Virginia Company created the House of Burgesses to enlist greater cooperation from the settlers and to make the colony more attractive to immigrants. The crown, when it took control, also recognized the need for the legislature to regulate tobacco production, encourage the development of other staples, finance government, and defend the colony.

Similarly, John Winthrop's clique could not govern Massachusetts without enlarging the terms of political participation. Town leaders refused to cooperate unless they had a share in the government. And Lord Baltimore likewise discovered that though the charter gave all power to the proprietor, he was too far away, and too ignorant of affairs in Maryland to enforce his will. He too had to solicit support from the settlers through a legislature.

Government intruded on the lives of most people mainly when it punished crime, levied taxes, settled disputes over land and debts, laid out roads, and constructed public facilities. As the population dispersed from the original points of settlement, local bodies arose to govern beyond the control of the authorities in Jamestown or Boston. Towns and counties administered by sheriffs and justices of the peace became the instruments of local government. In practice, local leaders were the men of wealth and standing in the neighborhood who had either enjoyed positions of prominence in England or, more likely, acquired them in America. The representatives of the counties and towns chosen to attend the legislature linked communities to the central government.

At the provincial capital sat the governor, appointed by the crown as in Virginia, by the proprietor as in Maryland, or elected by the freemen as in Massachusetts. A council, usually drawn from the most powerful local leaders, aided the executive, participated in law making as part of the assembly, and also served as a court of appeals. Harmonious relations between the governor and his council, and between both of them and the legislature required accommodation on all sides. A governor who antagonized the council and the local elite usually did not last. Secure tenure rested on the ability to win over powerful local men by giving them lucrative appointments, land grants, control of the fur trade, and other privileges. Governors learned that they needed the support of local officials to obtain cooperation from the legislature and council.

Local government assumed far greater importance and authority than in England where organs of central administration, developed over many centuries, had encroached upon local authority. In the absence of professionally staffed royal courts, county courts in America assumed broad jurisdiction, dispensing justice tempered by common sense and local political circumstance rather than in strict accordance with legal precedent or complex legal practices. The English sheriff, the king's man, had had his power curbed by a Parliament jealous of royal authority; in the colonies the sheriff owed his office to the local elite who sat as justices on the county court. In England serving as sheriff was often regarded as a burden; but in the colonies it was a lucrative post which the justices rotated among themselves. Town and county cliques influenced appointments to local government, thereby enabling them to perpetuate their power. Represented by one of their members in the legislature and sometimes in the council, controlling the militia and other offices, they had extensive autonomy, with little fear of intrusion from royal government.

As the governor learned to work with the most powerful native elements, incorporating them into his council, demands arose to remove the councillors from the assemblies into a separate house. Bicameralism, or a two house legislature, grew out of distinctions arising among governing groups and the desire to check the power of the governor and his supporters in the council.

For the most part, provincial authority remained remote whereas local government more closely affected people's lives. As long as settlers had to invest most of their energies in carving out settlements, clearing the land, cultivating new farms, setting up shops, developing trade, and relying on their own efforts, government played a lesser role in their lives than it did later. During the last quarter of the seventeenth century, however, widespread civil disturbances disrupted the peace and brought turmoil to colonial America, as people violently challenged established authority.

Sources of Instability

Between 1676 and 1688 rebellions erupted in half a dozen colonies from Massachusetts to North Carolina. These explosions occurred both because of pressures building up within colonial society and from external sources. As societies matured, rivalries among colonists intensified and compromise became increasingly difficult. At the same time, England, which had earlier paid little attention to the colonies, now attempted to tighten control.

Bacon's Rebellion in Virginia (1676) grew out of internal conflicts with a long-entrenched faction around Governor William Berkeley which enriched itself through control of numerous offices, grants of land, and domination of the fur trade. Planters excluded from the governor's favored circle were resentful over poor tobacco crops and low prices. The governor's handling of the Indians increased the discontent and touched off the explosion.

Virginians had broken the power of the local Indians a generation earlier and, by the 1670s, whites greatly outnumbered the nearby tribes. The Indians living along the edges of white settlements were pacified and friendly, encouraging planters to encroach further on Indian territory. As tension mounted, the whites became more aggressive in the face of Indian weakness, an experience repeated on countless frontiers for almost three centuries. When a planter stole some Indian property and Indians retaliated by stealing some hogs, both sides began murdering one another.

The stage was set for war. Eager to keep the peace, Governor Berkeley ordered whites to withdraw from exposed plantations behind a line of forts at the falls of the rivers. Friendly Indians were disarmed but supplied with necessities, and the sale of arms and munitions to Indians was banned. Accusing the governor of being "soft" on Indians, of appeasing bloodthirsty savages, abandoning frontier plantations, and preventing the westward expansion of whites, a group of planters, led by Nathaniel Bacon, attacked the friendly Indians.

Bacon had recently fled from England in disgrace. A cousin-in-law of Berkeley, he became a councillor and received a land grant on the frontier to which he retreated, becoming the champion of anti-Berkeley elements. When the governor refused to approve the actions of Bacon and his followers, they marched on Jamestown and forced a commission from him at gun point. Civil war broke out. Bacon captured the capitol and burned it to the ground. When he died suddenly in August, 1676, Berkeley crushed the resistance and executed twenty-three rebels.

The crown dispatched commissioners to restore peace, hoping to assure a continued flow of revenue from tobacco taxes. Believing that the Baconians enjoyed popular support, the commissioners insisted on leniency for the rebels. Many of the laws adopted by the legislature under rebel influence remained in force, reducing the influence of Berkeley's faction and opening new opportunities for those previously excluded by the dominant elite.

Bacon's rebellion proved that no group could hold power indefinitely unless it accommodated and admitted ambitious newer elements. The clique that formed around Governor Berkeley had become dominant during the second generation of settlement. By the 1670s, as population grew and settlement expanded, new families demanded a share in government. Recognition of their demands restored peace to the colony for another century.

Massachusetts, like Virginia, also overthrew a royal governor. Rebellion in the Bay colony grew out of new pressures from England that sharpened existing divisions within the province. After twenty years of civil war which saw the execution of Charles I and the establishment of a republic (1649–1660) headed by Oliver Cromwell, the Stuart dynasty reclaimed the throne. After the Restoration, the crown took an increasing interest in its American empire. It discharged obligations to followers by chartering new proprietary colonies in the Carolinas and Pennsylvania and it enacted mercantilist legislation to drive the Dutch from imperial commerce and channel trade to England.

The Puritan colonies in New England attracted particular attention because they had sympathized with Cromwell's regime and had persecuted Anglicans. In 1664 four commissioners arrived in New England to obtain aid against the Dutch, insure enforcement of the navigation acts and compliance with other English laws, and to stop Puritan persecution of religious dissenters. Chronic defiance by Massachuetts eventually led to the annulment of the original charter in 1684. The crown replaced Puritan government with the Dominion of New England (1685–1688) which brought Massachusetts, Rhode Island, and Connecticut under the control of a royal governor and contemplated the inclusion of New York, New Jersey, and Pennsylvania to centralize colonial defense against the French and to enforce the navigation acts.

At first the new regime enjoyed support from merchants, moderate Calvinists, and dissenters excluded from power by the Puritan elite. They looked to the crown to protect their interests, to give them a share in governing, and to relieve them from religious disabilities. In 1686, King James II dispatched Sir

Edmund Andros to take command of the dominion. The governor and a handpicked council of sympathetic merchants and dissenters ruled in place of the Massachusetts assembly. Furthermore, Andros declared that all land titles had to be reconfirmed subject to quitrent. He moved against illegal trade, permitted town meetings to be held only once a year, levied new taxes, seized control of the militia, and eliminated the religious privileges of Puritans.

In 1688 the Glorious Revolution in England overthrew the Stuart dynasty. James II's Catholicism alienated powerful interests who replaced him on the throne with William of Orange, a Dutch Protestant. Massachusetts Puritans seized the opportunity to denounce Andros as a supporter of James II and an intriguer with the pope and the French to deliver English Protestants to Catholic tyranny. When Bostonians took up arms, Andros found himself isolated. The moderates who had once welcomed the intrusion of English authority deserted him, since the governor had ignored them in favor of a small clique that monopolized privilege and threatened the property and commerce of others. Those remaining loyal to Andros were mostly new arrivals from England, and many joined him in jail.

Though the Puritan elite regained power, the crown refused to restore the old charter. It issued a new one in 1691 which gave the king power to review legislation and appoint the governor, authorized the Massachusetts legislature to elect the council subject to the governor's veto, substituted a property qualification for voting in place of church membership, and required toleration of all Protestants. Under this new arrangement peace returned to the Bay colony. The Puritan elite lost its power monopoly but still remained the dominant element and English authority gained a foothold. The crown abandoned the dominion scheme, permitting Rhode Island and Connecticut to be governed under their original charters and relied thereafter on persuasion and cajolery to obtain colonial cooperation against the French. Over sixty years passed before England made another attempt to unify the administration of the colonies.

The Glorious Revolution in England touched off rebellion elsewhere in the colonies. Maryland Protestants had long nursed complaints against the proprietors who, together with their Catholic relatives and favorites, monopolized offices, the Indian trade, and accumulated vast land holdings. Discontent in Maryland drew support from respectable "outsiders," merchants, justices of the peace, militia leaders, and planters in the newly developed regions where proprietary influences were weakest. When the Baltimore family failed to rush to the support of the new Protestant line in England, their Maryland antagonists overthrew them in the name of William of Orange. They established the Anglican church and Maryland became a royal colony for almost twenty-five years. In 1715 the crown restored the colony to Charles, 4th Lord Baltimore, a Protestant.

The revolt in Boston against the Dominion of New England also inspired rebellion in New York in 1689. Jacob Leisler, a Dutch merchant, organized discontented elements and overthrew the Andros regime. Leisler found support among New England settlers on Long Island and among the Dutch who were restless under English rule. Leisler appealed to a broad spectrum of artisans, merchants, and farmers alienated by an officeholding elite and their mercantile and landed allies who governed the province for their own benefit.

The Leislerians, not a rabble, included local leaders, church elders, merchants, and militia officers. They established order, removed Catholics from office, raised taxes, opened the courts, reestablished the assembly, and fought the Indians and the French. In 1691 a new royal governor arrived but Leisler resisted until finally forced to surrender. He and a lieutenant were convicted of treason and were executed.

The rebellions of the late seventeenth century revealed the growing complexity of colonial society. First and second generation settlers who were most successful at accumulating wealth and entrenching themselves in positions of privilege antagonized the ambitious but excluded elements. The disgruntled were unwilling to permit a few to use the state to secure permanent advantage. They came from diverse social origins—Anglicans in Massachusetts, Dutch and New Englanders in New York, Protestants in Maryland, frontier gentry in Virginia, and farmers, merchants, and artisans bound together by a growing sense of exclusion and disadvantage.

Long-standing European patterns of privilege seemed illegitimate in America; those enjoying them were unable to justify them. In the colonies preferment was something achieved through hard work, rather than by inheritance. Others willing to work just as hard demanded an equal opportunity to participate in government. The ease with which rebellious elements overthrew governments demonstrated the fragile nature of political authority in America. Its control rested more on the willingness of people to obey than on the use of force. Rulers learned they must accommodate the governed, if they wished to retain power and preserve peace.

The fate of the Dominion of New England taught similar lessons in England. In addition to the internal tensions generating rebellion, new pressures came from a crown eager to establish a tighter grip on its colonies, extract more wealth, and make defense secure. The new bands of royal officials sent to America quickly discovered that they lacked power to impose their will. Few in number, isolated from all but a favored clique of colonists, without military forces to back them up, royal officials eventually had to come to terms with American leaders.

In a fit of centralizing zeal, the crown in the late seventeenth century attempted to set aside the proprietary and corporate charters and turn them into royal colonies. These efforts failed. Both the proprietaries and corporate colonies fought back and with concessions managed to preserve a large degree of private power. In the course of defending themselves against English encroachment, Americans learned how to manipulate the levers of power in London and how to enter into satisfactory and profitable relationships with royal officials. The tendencies of this political system took clearer shape in the last seventy-five years of the colonial period.

The Structure of Colonial Politics in the Eighteenth Century

On a Sunday in midwinter (1750), the 101st anniversary of the execution of King Charles I, the minister of a fashionable Boston church advised his parishioners "that no civil rulers are to be obeyed when they enjoy things inconsistent with the words and command of God" nor should men submit to government "at the expense of that which is the great and sole end of government, the common good and welfare of society." A quarter century after Jonathan Mayhew preached his sermon against "unlimited Submission and Nonresistance to the Higher Power," Americans took up arms against their king, defending, they believed, their rights and human liberty. Justifying their revolution as a struggle to preserve self-government, the colonists thought they were upholding freedoms established during a century-and-a-half of settlement.

Mayhew's sharp warning against tyranny underscored the fact that the colonists enjoyed unusual scope in governing themselves. The distance and weakness of British authority enabled Americans to develop working institutions and traditions of self-government. But these arrangements evolved without plan and were outside the sanction of the formal constitution which supposedly governed England and its colonies.

From the beginning, the king had primary responsibility for colonial government. He granted and annulled charters, appointed royal governors, and had to supervise colonial development. Though the crown had relied initially on private enterprise to plant colonies, by the middle of the eighteenth century it had assumed control of all but five of the thirteen colonies. Parliament regulated trade according to mercantilist principles but the king enforced the laws. During the Restoration, Charles II (1660–1685) and James II (1685–1688) attempted to centralize administration. The Privy Council, the king's chief administrative body, established fact-finding committees to advise the crown on colonial affairs.

Because of more pressing matters at home and in Europe, no permanent government body administered the colonies. In 1696, the Board of Trade was created. Pressure to establish the Board of Trade came principally from those interested in a colonial economic development which would assure the primacy of British interests. The board advised the Privy Council on commercial questions, helped frame instructions to royal governors, and reviewed colonial legislation. But it did not have executive power. Moreover it had to compete with other agencies of the royal bureaucracy, such as the Admiralty, the Treasury, and the Secretary of State, for control of colonial affairs. The board's effectiveness varied with the involvement and competence of its membership. Many of its members showed little interest in its business, ignoring conditions in the colonies. This failure of the board to develop into an effective organ for imperial control, reflected a general indifference in Britain to strengthening control over the colonies, despite the wishes of the crown and some political leaders. Prosperity, at home *and* in the colonies, provided the best measure of success for a mercantilist empire. The empire's growing wealth confirmed the wisdom of allowing a loose rein to distant but profitable settlements. Tightening British control might provoke controversy in Parliament or in the colonies, reactions neither the king nor his ministers desired. It was much easier and cheaper to let colonists control their own affairs, just as it had seemed wise to employ private rather than public enterprise to establish colonies in the first place. Effective English control would have required the creation of a larger expensive colonial bureaucracy in America and England, and a permanent commitment of troops to defend the colonies.

Americans themselves shouldered these responsibilities in peacetime, through the militia, relying on British regulars in time of full-scale war. Financing an adequate civil service and military force raised some difficult questions. The king could not tax, but Parliament had never taxed colonists in the seventeenth century either and to do so after they had grown accustomed to self-taxation was politically dangerous. Nor could the Americans be counted on to contribute voluntarily to the royal treasury. So long as the colonies grew rapidly, and their increasing exports enabled them to remain Britain's best customer, prudence dictated to "let sleeping dogs lie," a maxim favored by Sir Robert Walpole, the king's "prime minister," and a leading figure in British government between 1721 and 1742. After the turbulence of civil war, Restoration, and a Glorious Revolution, England enjoyed political stability and rapid economic growth, and none wished to disturb things.

In these circumstances politicians preferred peace to reform. Moreover, few entirely appreciated the extent to which the Americans had chipped away at British power in America. The colonial elites and their instruments of government grew in influence and self-confidence, often silently undermining British authority. Americans did not challenge directly the theory of the constitution under which king and Parliament were sovereign. This was unnecessary so long as colonists succeeded in a long war of attrition and evasion against external control.

Until the 1760s not even the Americans, let alone Britons, realized how much their conceptions of sovereignty had diverged. Consequently, lack of royal control during the formative years of settlement, compounded by the ineffectiveness of later attempts to strengthen it, left king and Parliament supreme only in theory. As long as Americans could get their way by manipulation they did not challenge the notion of British supremacy. But well before the revolutionary crisis they were aware that government rests on the consent of the governed.

The principal instruments of self-government were the colonial legislatures. Their rise illuminates the process of political development in America. In the seventeenth century the councils, the local elite, together with the governor, usually dominated provincial politics. As colonial society became more complex and as additional settlements opened up, new fortunes were made and new families became prominent. The council could not find places for all these ambitious aspirants. Many looked to the lower house as the arena in which they could best advance their interests. As a result, the governors found it increasingly difficult to manage affairs by reaching accommodations with councillors' cliques, who in turn were losing their influence over the lower house. From advisory bodies without the power to initiate law—established initially on the sufferance of the crown or the proprietors—the lower houses persistently enlarged their influence until by the end of the colonial period they had become the most powerful branch of government.

Britons regarded the colonial legislatures as subordinate bodies created by higher authority and subject to external control, but Americans ran assemblies like miniature parliaments. Through persistent effort they assumed the power to control provincial finance and taxation, to pay the salaries of royal officials, and to issue paper money and like Parliament they regulated their own membership and internal business. Assemblies sometimes went beyond Parliament's power, encroaching further on the executive jurisdiction by appointing certain important officials and depriving the governor of patronage.

The legislature's chief antagonist in their quest for power was the governor, the king's or the proprietor's stand-in. As the colony's chief executive, he lacked both the power and the prestige which enabled the king and his ministers in England to manage Parliament. The governor had formidable responsibilities: to defend the royal interests and enforce British law, protect his colony against attack, and at the same time promote harmony among the colonists. These tasks proved virtually impossible because he lacked the power to impose his will, nor could he count on colonial cooperation short of bowing to local pressures and demands that violated his instructions.

Governors, like other royal officials in America and England, expected to make money. Some purchased their offices, at a high cost, from persons unwilling to emigrate. Officials soon discovered that cooperation with the colonists was the surest way to profit from an office and accumulate fees and land grants. The governor's fear of removal should he antagonize powerful interests intensified the tendency to seek accommodation. In England enemies and rivals schemed to oust him. Disgruntled colonists sent agents to London to undermine the governor's position and to cooperate with the rivals who wanted his job.

A governor unable to administer his colony smoothly, one who stirred up opposition in America and England, became a political liability and was presumably unfit to handle his job.

Self-interest thus encouraged governors to give way to colonial demands. His lack of sufficient power to resist made a virtue of such a course. Britain relied on the colonists to pay the governors but no colony established adequate salaries. Governors and legislatures haggled chronically, but the colonists had the advantage because the executive could not force them to vote acceptable compensation and the crown proved unwilling to assume the burden.

Lacking financial independence, governors also lacked enough patronage to control influential colonial politicians. Officials in England filled many of the most lucrative American positions and the colonists also encroached on the governor's appointive power. Thus a governor responsible for enforcing the navigation laws had no power over customs officials chosen in England; and customs collectors who honestly attempted to enforce the trade laws encountered colonial judges and juries who repeatedly acquitted violators. Governors and collectors thus found it more prudent and profitable to ignore smuggling of French sugar into the colonies. American traders preferred to bribe royal officials rather than pay the tax, thus modestly increasing business expenses but maximizing profits.

Some governors learned their lessons slowly and only after much difficulty. For instance, Francis Nicholson, Governor of Virginia (1698–1705), who was reputed to be "so abusive in his words and actions as not only to treat our best gentlemen with scurrilous names of dogs, rogues, villains, dastards, cheats, and cowards," but also "our best women with the names of whores, bitches, jades, etc.," obviously had lost the confidence of his people. Although a governor *appeared* to have the ability to rule independently, his lack of financial security, the uncertainty of tenure, and a desire to profit from office taught him that accommodation was the path to success. A broadening of political participation which enabled a growing percentage of adult males to participate in government compounded his difficulties. Politics became more turbulent and democratic than in Britain.

In Britain the landed aristocracy and some of the most successful representatives of the merchant class dominated politics. Property qualifications kept most people from voting and facilitated parliamentary control by a few. Some of the titled families with extensive estates had several parliamentary seats in their pockets ("pocket" or "rotten" boroughs) and could also count on the support of friends and relatives among the gentry. Farmers, artisans, and tradespeople either played no role in elections or passively deferred to rule by their landlords and customers. Thus a small and controlled electorate enabled a landed and mercantile elite to rule.

The electorate in America was, relative to the total population, much larger. Many farmers had enough land to satisfy the property qualification for voting, which in England disfranchised most citizens. American voters also inclined toward deference to the large planters, wealthy merchants, and professionals, but it was much harder to control elections. The enlarged electorate retained the power to defy local magnates and once aroused it was too numerous to manipulate easily.

The structure of representation posed further obstacles. Members of Parliament represented counties and boroughs as they existed in medieval times when Parliament emerged. Areas that lost population over the centuries still kept their seats whereas other growing parts of the country that had not been represented in the Middle Ages sent no one to the House of Commons. For this reason families controlling rotten boroughs with few voters retained their power while expanding and important parts of the country remained unrepresented.

Such inequities were less common in America. There, legislative districts had to be created repeatedly. In Massachusetts each town, and in Virginia each county, sent delegates to the assembly. New towns and counties were usually represented along with the old. As the older counties and towns grew in population, they often split, each entitled to representatives. Representation roughly followed the distribution of population, and hence rotten boroughs did not develop, although in the eighteenth century newly settled areas complained of underrepresentation. Rapid growth in population and the extension of settlements into new areas regularly increased the size of the colonial assemblies as new members came from freshly created districts. The size of the body and newness of its members often made the assembly difficult to manage. A governor or a faction that attempted to buy off opposition found that the numbers that had to be appeased steadily grew.

No modern political parties existed in colonial America to arouse the voters, or to nominate candidates espousing rival programs and appealing for mass support. Because average citizens had not voted in Europe, many of those eligible in America showed no interest in politics. Most worked their farms or at their trades, leaving the management of public offices to their "betters."

Without parties, colonial ruling groups formed factions, loose groups of individuals temporarily allied to pursue immediate political advantage by obtaining lucrative offices, land grants, and contracts.

The governor had to navigate the dangerous waters of factional politics. He tried to win the support of the most powerful factions thereby hoping to influence the council and the legislature. But every time he made a friend, he also made an enemy. The governor could never accommodate everyone, nor could his supporters be certain of maintaining control. Factions out of power harassed the governor and his allies. The tendency of dominant factions to quarrel among themselves over the spoils created instability, and new alliances were formed. Moreover, as successful new groups emerged in trade, farming, or the professions, they too demanded political recognition. An apathetic electorate saw little opportunity for ordinary citizens to gain anything through politics. From time to time, however, voters reacted to threats to their interests or saw ways to benefit themselves politically. Baptists suffering religious disabilities in Virginia or Massachusetts, frontiersmen anxious over Indian depredations, farmers and merchants desiring paper money,

Scotch-Irish Presbyterians jealous of Quaker political control in Pennsylvania—these and other varied interests periodically entered politics. When interest groups engaged actively in politics, more people went to the polls contesting elections hotly, and campaigns involved issues, not simply rival personalities. But political involvement seldom lasted. Once a group had obtained a specific objective, it gave up the struggle, lapsed back into traditional apathy and left politics to the intrigue of factions.

The clash of factions and the periodic outbursts of aroused socioeconomic interests made colonial politics turbulent. More often than not, however, elections went uncontested; some communities even declined to be represented in order to save money. In most, self-perpetuating cliques of leading families held office and filled vacancies. "Go into every village in New England," John Adams once observed, "and you will find that the office of justice of the peace, and even the place of representative, which has ever depended only on the freest election of the people, have generally descended from generation to generation in three or four families at most." Ambitious and talented newcomers found it more prudent to serve an apprenticeship under the dominant gentry than to challenge it directly. Loyalty and faithful service usually earned advancement up the officeholding ladder. Sometimes, however, the ruling groups quarreled among themselves, or aspirants lacked patience to wait for recognition. If a county courthouse ring failed to repulse the challengers, a new faction took over.

Politics was more competitive in some colonies than in others. Politics in a colony whose population grew rapidly, pushing into new regions, and which was divided by ethnic, religious, and sectional interests, tended to be competitive. Pennsylvania politics, for instance, was competitive because it had a diverse social order with a great commercial center in Philadelphia balancing a large and rapidly growing rural hinterland. And numerous Quakers, Scotch-Irish, and Germans fought for political advantage. The division between supporters and opponents of the proprietors further heated up the colony's politics. In contrast, South Carolina politics remained relatively uncompetitive.

There a planter-merchant elite of large rice and indigo planters and Charleston merchants, mostly slave-owning Anglicans, ruled the province. Until 1760, the Indians kept whites from filling up the back country and bringing sectional, ethnic, religious, and economic diversity to the colony.

Where politicians competed, attitudes toward authority began to change. Government, originally conceived as an instrument to control human passions, became the object of contests for power. People began to view the state as an instrument for self-advancement. Those wielding power had triumphed at the polls or behind the scenes; they made no claim to a divine right to rule. The seed was being sown for the day when revolutionary Americans declared that "governments derive their just power from the consent of the governed."

The seed bore strange fruit in the case of John Peter Zenger, a New York newspaper editor, prosecuted in 1734–1735 for criticizing the governor but freed by a jury which disregarded English law. The law held that criticism of government was seditious since governments supposedly could not survive public attack. The New York jury insisted that because Zenger published the truth he was immune from punishment. This decision did not bind future courts and the American tradition of freedom of speech has roots much more complex than Zenger's case, but it pointed to the future when freedom of press came to be regarded as an indispensable condition of free government. English governors, fearful of antagonizing powerful local politicians, initiated few successful attacks on the press. Colonial legislatures, however, without similar restraints, were the principal enemies of a free press and often punished critics for contempt.

Though before the 1760s colonists had not yet defended popular sovereignty and freedom to criticize government, they were much less respectful of authority than were the first generations of settlers or their contemporaries in eighteenth century Europe. Tradition required that the humble members of society defer to rule by their social superiors. For the most part, Americans conformed. Subtly and slowly, however, habits of deference fell away in a social order lacking either a nobility or other familiar ruling elements. With wealth so abundant in America, shrewd and enterprising newcomers constantly climbed the ladder, forcing their way into prominence and edging aside established families. When members of the gentry competed for the votes of farmers and artisans, it became increasingly difficult to know to whom deference was due.

The Silent Revolution

In 1645, John Winthrop, recently defeated for reelection as governor of Massachusetts, lectured his people "about the authority of the magistrates and the liberty of the people." "It is you yourselves," he reminded them, "who have called us to this office, and, being called by you, we have our authority from God, . . . the contempt and violation whereof hath been vindicated with examples of divine vengeance." A century later, a Scottish physician traveling through the colonies reported that in Pennsylvania "their government is a kind of anarchy," in New Jersey "the House of Assembly . . . was chiefly composed of mechanicks and ignorant wretches, obstinate to the last degree" and in Rhode Island, government "is somewhat democratick" with royal officials afraid to "exercise their office for fear of the fury and unruliness of the people."

Slowly but steadily Americans fashioned political arrangements that differed from those brought from Europe or those which persisted in the Old World. King and Parliament remained supreme in theory, but the working constitution of the empire permitted Americans to carve out areas in which they were virtually self-governing. Yet few in England or America realized before the 1760s the tenuous nature of English authority nor how much independence Americans actually enjoyed. Within the colonies, small groups of leading citizens held power but with less security than their English counterparts. A larger electorate and unstable ruling groups, more easily penetrated and challenged, weakened authority whether exercised by the English or Americans and gave individuals greater scope to shape their own lives.

By the end of the colonial period white Americans were not only the most prosperous but also the freest people in the world. Men did not transplant intact the ways of the Old World to the New. In America they found freedom from English control and an abundance of resources that liberated individual energies, raised the level of aspiration, and enabled people to mold the world in which they lived. These efforts evolved into a new material and political order, as well as into a social order that became distinctly American.

Document: Colonial Politics and Freedom of the Press
Andrew Hamilton's Address to the Jury in the Case of John Peter Zenger

In 1735 John Peter Zenger, printer of the New York Weekly Journal, *was tried for seditious libel against the administration of Governor William Cosby. Andrew Hamilton, one of the leading lawyers in the colonies, defended Zenger and won an acquittal, delivering the extraordinary address to the jury reprinted below. The verdict flew in the face of British law and practice. It did not set a precedent for colonial courts or those of the young American republic following the Revolution, yet the Zenger trial is a portent of the development of popular government in the United States.*

The case grew out of the rivalry between Cosby and a faction surrounding the Morris family, a faction once powerful in New York politics but now alienated by Governor Cosby's alliance with its enemies. The Morrisites hired John Peter Zenger

Source: Livingston Rutherfurd, ed., *John Peter Zenger* (New York, 1904), pp. 74–78, 88–89, 93–101, 119–123.

to publish a newspaper as part of their campaign to drive Cosby
from office by stirring up popular discontent.

Cosby struck back by clamping Zenger in jail. According
to English law, a person was free to publish without being cen-
sored but was liable for criticism that jeopardized the security
or tranquillity of the state. Moreover, juries had only power to
determine the facts, that is, whether Zenger had published the
libel. The judge decided the law, whether the publication in
question was seditious. Hamilton made the novel argument that
truth was a defense; if Zenger's publication was true, Hamilton
argued, the jury must free him. This doctrine carried the day
because Cosbyites were unpopular, something which Hamilton
exploited. Because the law was against him, Hamilton of neces-
sity appealed to political theory. He tried to elevate an incident
which began as a quarrel between two self-seeking factions into
a battle involving fundamental principles of human liberty. A
generation later, when Americans resisted new British taxes and
controls, they also believed they were battling tyranny in defense
of the rights of man.

The Zenger case reveals the factious nature of colonial
politics, the vulnerability of royal governors to local attack, and
the American tendency to question settled English law and to
resort to basic principles of justice and free government in
defense of special interests.

Mr. *Hamilton.* May it please Your Honour; I agree with
Mr. Attorney, that Government is a sacred Thing, but I differ
very widely from him when he would insinuate, that the just
Complaints of a Number of Men, who suffer under a bad Administration, is libelling that Administration. Had I believed that to
be Law, I should not have given the Court the Trouble of hearing any Thing that I could say in this cause. I own, when I read
the Information,[1] I had not the Art to find out (without the
Help of Mr. Attorney's *Innuendo's*) that the Governor was the
Person meant in every Period of that News Paper; and I was

[1] An indictment brought by the state's attorney rather than by a
grand jury which, in this case, refused to indict Zenger.

inclined to believe, that they were wrote by some, who from an extraordinary Zeal for Liberty, had misconstrued the Conduct of some Persons in Authority into Crimes; and that Mr. Attorney out of his too great Zeal for Power, had exhibited this Information, to correct the Indiscretion of my Client; and at the same Time, to shew his Superiors the great Concern he had, lest they should be treated with any undue Freedom. But from what Mr. Attorney has just now said, *to wit*, That this Prosecution was directed by the Governour and Council, and from the extraordinary Appearance of People of all Conditions, which I observe in Court upon this Occasion, I have Reason to think, that those in the Administration have by this Prosecution some-thing more in View, and that the People believe they have a good deal more at Stake, than I apprehended: And therefore, as it is become my Duty, to be both plain and particular in this Cause, I beg Leave to bespeak the Patience of the Court.

I was in Hopes, as that terrible Court, where those dreadful Judgments were given, and that Law established, which Mr. Attorney has produced for Authorities to support this Cause, was long ago laid aside, as the most dangerous Court to the Liberties of the People of *England*, that ever was known in that Kingdom; that Mr. Attorney knowing this, would not have attempted to set up a Star-Chamber[2] here, nor to make their Judgments a Precedent to us: For it is well known, that what would have been judg'd Treason in those Days for a Man to speak, I think, has since not only been practiced as lawful, but the contrary Doctrine has been held to be Law. . . .

Is it not surprising to see a Subject, upon his receiving a Commission from the King to be a Governor of a Colony in *America*, immediately imagining himself to be vested with all the Prerogatives belonging to the sacred Person of his Prince? And which is yet more astonishing, to see that a People can be so wild as to allow of, and acknowledge those Prerogatives and

[2] The Court of Star Chamber, operating without the safeguard of jury trials was used by the crown in the sixteenth and seventeenth centuries to suppress religious and political dissent, and was especially infamous for its persecution of the Puritans and for its use of torture.

Exemptions, even to their own Destruction? Is it so hard a
Matter to distinguish between the Majesty of our Sovereign, and
the Power of a Governor of the Plantations? Is not this making
very free with our Prince, to apply that Regard, Obedience and
Allegiance to a Subject which is due only to Our Sovereign?
And yet in all the Cases which Mr. Attorney has cited, to show
the Duty and Obedience we owe to the Supreme Magistrate, it
is the King that is there meant and understood, tho' Mr. Attorney
is pleased to urge them as Authorities to prove the Heinousness
of Mr. *Zenger's* offence against the Governor of *New-York*. The
several Plantations are compared to so many large Corporations,
and perhaps not improperly; and can any one give an Instance,
that the Mayor or Head of a Corporation, ever put in a Claim
to the sacred Rights of Majesty? Let us not (while we are pre-
tending to pay a great Regard to our Prince and His Peace)
make bold to transfer that Allegiance to a Subject, which we
owe to our King only. What strange Doctrine is it, to press every
Thing for Law here which is so in *England*? I believe we should
not think it a Favour, at present at least, to establish this Practice. In *England* so great a Regard and Reverence is had to the
Judges, that if any man strike another in *Westminster Hall*,
while the Judges are sitting, he shall lose his Right Hand, and
forfeit his Land and Goods, for so doing. And tho' the Judges
here claim all the Powers and Authorities within this Government, that a Court of King's Bench has in *England*, yet I believe
Mr. Attorney will scarcely say, that such a Punishment could
be legally inflicted on a Man for committing such an Offence,
in the Presence of the Judges sitting in any Court within the
Province of *New-York*. The Reason is obvious; a Quarrel or Riot
in *New-York* cannot possibly be attended with those dangerous
Consequences that it might in *Westminster Hall*; nor (I hope)
will it be alledged, than any Misbehaviour to a Governor in the
Plantations will, or ought to be, judged of or punished, as a like
Undutifulness would be, to Our Sovereign. From all which, I
hope Mr. Attorney will not think it proper to apply his Law-
Cases (to support the Cause of his Governor) which have only
been judged, where the King's Safety or Honour was concerned.

It will not be denied but that a Freeholder in the Province of *New-York* has as good a Right to the sole and separate Use of his Lands, as a Freeholder in *England*, who has a Right to bring an Action of Trespass against his Neighbour, for suffering his Horse or Cow to come and feed upon his Land or eat his Corn, whether inclosed or not inclosed; and yet I believe it would be looked upon as a strange Attempt, for one Man here, to bring an Action against another, whose Cattle and Horses feed upon his Grounds not inclosed, or indeed for eating and treading down his Corn, if that were not inclosed. Numberless are the Instances of this Kind that might be given, to shew, that what is good Law at one Time and in one Place, is not so at another Time and in another Place; so that I think, the Law seems to expect, that in these Parts of the World Men should take Care, by a good Fence, to preserve their Property, from the Injury of unruly Beasts. And perhaps there may be as good Reason why Men should take the same Care, to make an honest and upright Conduct a Fence and Security against the Injury of unruly Tongues. . . .

Gentlemen of the Jury, it is to you we must now appeal, for Witness, to the Truth of the Facts we have offered, and are denied the Liberty to prove; and let it not seem strange, that I apply my self to you in this Manner, I am warranted so to do, both by Law and Reason. The Last supposes you to be summoned, *out of the Neighbourhood where the Fact is alleged to be committed;* and the Reason of your being taken out of the Neighbourhood is, *because you are supposed to have the best Knowledge of the fact that is to be tried.* And were you to find a Verdict against my client, you must take upon you to say, the Papers referred to in the Information, and which we acknowledge we printed and published, are *false, scandalous and seditious:* but of this I can have no Apprehension. You are Citizens of *New-York;* you are really what the Law supposes you to be, *honest and lawful Men;* and, according to my Brief, the Facts which we offer to prove were not committed in a Corner; they are notoriously known to be true; and therefore in your Justice lies our Safety. And as we are denied the Liberty of giving Evidence, to prove the Truth of what we have published, I will beg Leave to lay it down as a standing Rule in such Casess, *That the suppressing of Evidence ought always to be taken for the strongest Evidence;* and I hope it will have that Weight with you. . . .

I know, may it please Your Honour, the Jury may do so; but I do likewise know, they may do otherwise. I know they have the Right beyond all Dispute, to determine both the Law and the Fact, and where they do not doubt of the Law, they ought to do so. This of leaving it to the Judgment of the Court, *whether the Words are libellous or not*, in Effect renders Juries useless (to say no worse) in many Cases; but this I shall have Occasion to speak to by and by; and I will with the Court's Leave proceed to examine the Inconveniences that must inevitably arise from the Doctrines Mr. Attorney has laid down; and I observe, in support of this Prosecution, he has frequently repeated the Words taken from the Case of *Libel, famosus*, in 5 *Co.* This is indeed the leading case, and to which almost all the other Cases upon the Subject of Libels do refer; and I must insist upon saying, That according as this Case seems to be understood by the [Court] and Mr. Attorney, it is not Law at this Day: For thou' I own it to be base and unworthy to scandalize any Man, yet I think it is even villanous to scandalize a Person of publick Character, and I will go so far into Mr. Attorney's Doctrine as to agree, that if the faults, Mistakes, nay even the Vices of such a Person be private and personal, and don't affect the Peace of the Publick, or the Liberty or Property of our Neighbour, it is unmanly and unmannerly to expose them either by Word or Writing. But when a Ruler of the People brings his personal Failings, but much more his Vices, into his Administration, and the People find themselves affected by them, either in their Liberties or Properties, that will alter the Case mightily, and all the high Things that are said in Favour of Rulers, and of Dignities, and upon the side of Power, will not be able to stop People's Mouths when they feel themselves oppressed, I mean in a free Government. It is true in Times past it was a crime to speak Truth, and in that terrible Court of Star Chamber, many worthy and brave Men suffered for so doing; and yet even in that Court, and in those bad Times, a great and good Man durst say, what I hope will not be taken amiss of me to say in this Place, *to wit, The Practice of informations for Libels is a Sword in the Hands of a wicked King, and an arrant Coward, to cut down and destroy the innocent; the one cannot, because of his high Station, and the other dares not, because of his want of Courage, revenge himself in another Manner. . . .*

. . . All Men agree that we are governed by the best of Kings, and I cannot see the Meaning of Mr. Attorney's Caution; my well known Principles, and the Sense I have of the Blessings we enjoy under His present Majesty, makes it impossible for me to err, and I hope, even to be suspected, in that Point of Duty to my King. May it please Your Honour, I was saying, That notwithstanding all the Duty and Reverence claimed by Mr. Attorney to Men in Authority, they are not exempt from observing the Rules of Common Justice, even in their private or public Capacities; the Laws of our Mother Country know no Exemption. It is true, Men in Power are harder to be come at for Wrongs they do, either to a private Person, or to the Publick; especially a Governor in the Plantations, where they insist upon an Exemption from answering Complaints of any Kind in their own Government. We are indeed told, and it is true they are obliged to answer a Suit in the King's Courts at *Westminster*, for a Wrong done to any Person here: But do we not know how impracticable this is to most Men among us, to leave their Families (who depend upon their Labour and Care for their Livelihood) and carry Evidences to *Britain*, and at a great, nay, a far greater Expense than almost any of us are able to bear, only to prosecute a Governour for an Injury done here. But when the Oppression is general, there is no Remedy even that Way, no, our Constitution has (blessed be God) given us an Opportunity, if not to have such Wrongs redressed, yet by our Prudence and Resolution we may in a great Measure prevent the committing of such Wrongs, by making a Governour sensible that it is to his interest to be just to those under his Care; for such is the Sense that Men in General (I mean Freemen) have of common Justice, that when they come to know, that a chief Magistrate abuses the Power with which he is trusted, for the good of the People, and is attempting to turn that very Power against the Innocent, whether of high or low degree, I say, Mankind in general seldom fail to interpose, and as far as they can, prevent the Destruction of their fellow Subjects. And has it not often been seen (and I hope it will always be seen) that when the Representatives of a free People are by just Representations or Remonstrances, made sensible of the Sufferings of their Fellow-Subjects, by the Abuse of Power in the Hands of a Governour, they have declared (and loudly too) that they were not obliged by any Law to support a Governour who goes about to destroy a Province or Colony, or their Priviledges, which by His Majesty he was appointed, and by the Law he is bound to protect and encourage. But I pray it may be considered of what Use is this mighty Priviledge, if every Man that suffers must be silent? And if a Man must be taken up as a Libeller, for telling his Sufferings to his Neighbour? I know it may be answer'd, *Have you not a Legislature? Have you not a House of Representatives, to whom you may complain?* And to this I answer, we have. But what then? Is an Assembly to be troubled with every Injury done by a Governour? Or are they to hear of nothing but what those in the Administration will please to tell them? Or what Sort of a Tryal must a Man have? And how is he to be remedied; especially if the Case were, as I have known it to happen in *America* in my Time; That a Governour who has Places (I will not [say] Pensions, for I believe they seldom give that to another which they can take to themselves) to bestow, and can or will keep the same Assembly (after he has modeled them so as to get a Majority of the House in his Interest) for near *twice Seven Years* together? I pray, what Redress is to be expected for an honest Man, who makes his Complaint against a Governour to an Assembly who may properly enough be said, to be made by the same Governour against whom the Complaint is made? The Thing answers it self. No, it is natural, it is a Priviledge, I will go farther, it is a Right which all Freemen claim, and are entitled to complain when they are hurt; they have a Right pub-

lickly to remonstrate the Abuses of Power, in the strongest
Terms, to put their Neighbours upon their Guard, against the
Craft or open Violence of Men in Authority, and to assert with
Courage the Sense they have of the Blessings of Liberty, the
Value they put upon it, and their Resolution at all Hazards to
preserve it, as one of the greatest Blessings Heaven can bestow.
And when a House of Assembly composed of honest Freemen
sees the general Bent of the Peoples Inclinations, That is it
which must and will (I'm sure it ought to) weigh with a Legislature, in Spite of all the Craft, Caressing and Cajolling, made
use of by a Governour, to divert them from hearkening to the
Voice of their Country. As we all very well understand the true
Reason, why Gentlemen take so much Pains and make such
great Interest to be appointed Governours, so is the Design of
their Appointment not less manifest. We know his Majesty's
gracious Intentions to his Subjects; he desires no more than that
his People in the Plantations should be kept up to their Duty
and Allegiance to the crown of *Great Britain*, that Peace may
be preserved amongst them, and Justice impartially administered; that we may be governed so as to render us useful
to our Mother Country, by encouraging us to make and raise
such Commodities as may be useful to *Great Britain*. But will
any one say, that all or any of these good Ends are to be effected,
by a Governour's setting his People together by the Ears, and by
the Assistance of one Part of the People to plague and plunder
the other? The Commission which Governours bear, while they
execute the Powers given them, according to the Intent of the
Royal Grantor, expressed in their Commissions, requires and
deserves very great Reverence and Submission; but when a
Governour departs from the Duty enjoined him by his Sovereign, and acts as if he was less accountable than the Royal Hand
that gave him all that Power and Honour which he is possessed
of; this sets People upon examining and enquiring into the
Power, Authority and Duty of such a Magistrate, and to com-
pare those with his Conduct, and just as far as they find he
exceeds the Bounds of his Authority, or falls short in doing
impartial Justice to the People under his Administration, so far

they very often, in return, come short in their Duty to such a Governour. For Power alone will not make a Man beloved, and I have heard it observed, That the Man who was neither good nor wise before his being made a Governour, never mended upon his Preferment, but has been generally observed to be worse; For Men who are not endued with Wisdom and Virtue, can only be kept in Bounds by the Law; and by how much the further they think themselves out of the Reach of the Law, by so much the more wicked and cruel Men are. I wish there were no Instances of the Kind at this Day. And wherever this happens to be the Case of a Governour, unhappy are the People under his Administration, and in the End he will find himself so too; for the People will neither love him nor support him. I make no Doubt but there are those here, who are zealously concerned for the Success of this Prosecution, and yet I hope they are not many, and even some of those, I am perswaded (when they consider what Length such Prosecutions may be carried, and how deeply the Liberties of the People may be affected by such Means) will not all abide by their present Sentiments; I say, *Not All:* For the Man who from an Intimacy and Acquaintance with a Governour has conceived a personal Regard for him, the Man who has felt none of the Strokes of his Power, the Man who believes that a Governour has a Regard for him and confides in him, it is natural for such Men to wish well to the Affairs of such a Governour; and as they may be Men of Honour and Generosity, may, and no Doubt will, wish him Success, so far as the Rights and the Priviledges of their Fellow Citizens are not affected. But as Men of Honour, I can apprehend nothing from them; they will never exceed that Point. There are others who are under stronger Obligations, and those are such, as are in some Sort engaged in Support of a Governour's Cause, by their own or their Relations Dependance on his Favour, for some Post or Preferment; such Men have what is commonly called Duty and Gratitude, to influence their Inclinations, and oblige them to go to his Lengths. I know Men's Interests are very near to them, and they will do much, rather than foregoe the Favour of a Governour, and a Livelihood at the same Time; but I can with very just Grounds hope, even from those Men, whom I will suppose to be Men of Honour and Conscience too, that when they see, the Liberty of their Country is in Danger, either by their Concurrence, or even by their Silence, they will like *Englishmen*, and like themselves, freely make a Sacrifice of any Preferment or Favour rather than be accessory to destroying the Liberties of their Country, and entailing Slavery upon their Posterity. There are indeed another set of Men, of whom I have no Hopes, I mean such, who lay aside all other Considerations, and are ready to joyn with Power in any Shapes, and with any Man or Sort of Men, by whose Means or Interest they may be assisted to gratify their Malice and Envy against those whom they have been pleased to hate; and that have no other Reason, but because they are Men of Abilities and Integrity, or at least are possessed of some valuable Qualities far superior to their own. But as Envy is the Sin of the Devil, and therefore very hard, if at all, to be repented of, I will believe there are but few of this detestable and worthless Sort of Men, nor will their Opinions or Inclinations have any Influence upon this Tryal. But to proceed; I beg Leave to insist, That the Right of complaining or remonstrating is natural; And the Restraint upon this natural Right is the Law only, and that those Restraints can only extend to what is *false;* For as it is Truth alone which can excuse or justify any Man for complaining of a bad Administration, I as frankly agree, that nothing ought to excuse a Man who raises a false Charge or Accusation, even against a private Person, and that no manner of Allowance ought to be made to him who does so against a publick Magistrate. *Truth* ought to govern the whole Affair of Libels, and yet the Party accused runs Risque enough even then; for if he fails of proving every Tittle of what he has wrote, and to the Satisfaction of the Court and Jury too, he may find to his Cost, that when the Prosecution is set on Foot by Men in Power, it seldom wants Friends to Favour it. . . .

Gentlemen [of the jury]: The Danger is great, in Proportion to the Mischief that may happen, through our too great Credulity. A proper Confidence in a Court is commendable; but as the

Verdict (whatever it is) will be yours, you ought to refer no Part of your Duty to the Discretion of other Persons. If you should be of Opinion, that there is no Falsehood in Mr. *Zenger's* Papers, you will, nay (pardon me for the Expression) you ought to say so; because you don't know whether others (I mean the Court) may be of that Opinion. It is your Right to do so, and there is much depending upon your Resolution, as well as upon your Integrity.

The loss of liberty to a generous Mind, is worse than Death; and yet we know there have been those in all Ages, who for the sake of Preferment, or some imaginary Honour, have freely lent a helping Hand, to oppress, nay to destroy their Country. This brings to my Mind that saying of the immortal *Brutus*, when he looked upon the Creatures of *Cæsar*, who were very great Men, but by no Means good Men. *"You* Romans *said* Brutus, *if yet I may call you so, consider* "what you are doing; remember that you are assisting Cæsar *to forge those very Chains, which one Day he will make your selves wear."* This is what every Man (that values Freedom) ought to consider: He should act by Judgment and not by Affection or Self-Interest; for, where those prevail, No Ties of either Country or Kindred are regarded, as upon the other Hand, the Man, who loves his Country, prefers it's Liberty to all other Considerations, well knowing that without Liberty, life is a Misery.

A famous Instance of this is found in the History of another brave *Roman* of the same Name, I mean *Lucius Junius Brutus*, whose story is well known and therefore I shall mention no more of it, than only to shew the Value he put upon the Freedom of his Country. After this great Man, with his Fellow Citizens whom he had engag'd in the Cause, had banish'd *Tarquin* the Proud, the last King of *Rome*, from a Throne which he ascended by inhuman Murders and possess'd by the most dreadful Tyranny and Proscriptions, and had by this Means, amass'd incredible Riches, even sufficient to bribe to his Interest, many of the young Nobility of *Rome*, to assist him in recovering the Crown; but the Plot being discover'd, the principal Conspirators were apprehended, among whom were two of the Sons of *Junius Brutus*.

It was absolutely necessary that some should be made Examples of, to deter others from attempting the restoring of *Tarquin* and destroying the Liberty of *Rome*. And to effect this it was, that *Lucius Junius Brutus*, one of the Consuls of *Rome*, in the Presence of the *Roman* People, sat Judge and condemned his own Sons, as Traitors to their Country: And to give the last Proof of his exalted Virtue, and his Love of Liberty: He with a Firmness of Mind (only becoming so great a Man) caus'd their Heads to be struck off in his own Presence; and when he observ'd that his rigid Virtue, occasion'd a sort of Horror among the People, it is observ'd he only said, *"My Fellow-Citizens, do not think that "this Proceeds from any Want of natural Affection: No, The "Death of the Sons of* Brutus *can affect* Brutus *only; but the loss "of Liberty will affect my Country."* Thus highly was Liberty esteem'd in those Days that a Father could sacrifice his Sons to save his Country. But why do I go to Heathen *Rome*, to bring Instances of the Love of Liberty, the best Blood of *Britain* has been shed in the Cause of Liberty; and the Freedom we enjoy at this Day, may be said to be (in great measure) owing to the glorious Stand the famous *Hamden*, and others of our Countrymen, made against the arbitrary Demands, and illegal Impositions, of the Times in which they lived; Who rather than give up the Rights of *Englishmen*, and submit to pay an illegal Tax of no more, I think, than 3 Shillings, resolv'd to undergo, and for their Liberty of their Country did undergo the greatest Extremities, in that arbitrary and terrible Court of Star Chamber, to whose arbitrary Proceedings, (it being compos'd of the Principal Men of the Realm, and calculated to support arbitrary Government) no Bounds or Limits could be set, nor could any other Hand remove the Evil but a Parliament.

Power may justly be compared to a great River, while kept within its due Bounds, is both Beautiful and Useful; but when it overflows it's Banks, it is then too impetuous to be stemm'd, it bears down all before it, and bring Destruction and Desolation wherever it comes. If then this is the Nature of Power, let us at least do our Duty, and like wise Men (who value Freedom) use our utmost care to support Liberty, the only Bulwark against lawless Power, which in all Ages has sacrificed to its wild Lust and boundless Ambition, the Blood of the best Men that ever liv'd.

I hope to be pardon'd Sir for my Zeal upon this Occasion; it is an old and wise Caution, *That when our Neighbours House is on Fire, we ought to take Care of our own.* For tho' Blessed be God, I live in a Government where Liberty is well understood, and freely enjoy'd; yet Experience has shewn us all (I'm sure it has to me) that a bad Precedent in one Government, is soon set up for an Authority in another; and therefore I cannot but think it mine, and every Honest Man's Duty, that (while we pay all due Obedience to Men in Authority) we ought at the same Time to be upon our Guard against Power, wherever we apprehend that it may affect ourselves or our Fellow-Subjects.

I am truely very unequal to such an Undertaking on many Accounts. And you see I labour under the Weight of many Years, and am born down with great Infirmities of Body; yet Old and Weak as I am, I should think it my Duty, if required, to go to the utmost Part of the Land, where my Service could be of any Use in assisting to quench the Flame of Prosecutions upon Informations, set on Foot by the Government, to deprive a People of the Right of Remonstrating (and complaining too) of the arbitrary Attempts of Men in Power. Men who injure and oppress the People under their Administration provoke them to cry out and complain; and then make that very Complaint the Foundation for new Oppressions and Prosecutions. I wish I could say there were no Instances of this Kind. But to conclude; the Question before the Court and you, Gentlemen of the Jury, is not of small nor private Concern, it is not the Cause of a poor Printer, nor of *New-York* alone, which you are now trying: No! It may in its Consequence, affect every Freeman that lives under a British Government on the main of *America.* It is the best Cause. It is the Cause of Liberty; and I make no Doubt but your upright Conduct, this Day, will not only entitle you to the Love and Esteem of your Fellow-Citizens; but every Man who prefers Freedom to a Life of Slavery will bless and honour You, as Men who have baffled the Attempt of Tyranny; and by an impartial and uncorrupt Verdict, have laid a noble Foundation for securing to ourselves, our Posterity, and our Neighbours, That, to which Nature and the Laws of our Country have given us a Right—The Liberty—both of exposing and opposing arbitrary Power (in these Parts of the World, at least) by speaking and writing Truth.

Suggestions for Further Reading

Political Development

Bernard Bailyn, *The Origins of American Politics* (1968); J. R. Pole, *Political Representation in England and the Origins of the American Republic* (1966); Jack P. Greene, *The Quest for Power: The Lower Houses of Assembly in the Southern Royal Colonies, 1689–1776* (1963); Leonard W. Labaree, *Royal Government in America* (1930); Charles S. Sydnor, *American Revolutionaries in the Making* (1965)*; *The Glorious Revolution in America*, Michael G. Hall, et al., eds., (1964)*; L. W. Labaree, *Conservatism in Early American History* (1948), chap. 1*; J. R. Pole, "Historians and the Problem of Early American Democracy," *American Historical Review*, vol. 67 (1962), pp. 626–646; *Politics and Society in Colonial America*, Michael G. Kammen ed., (1968)*.

The South

Leonidas Dodson, *Alexander Spotswood, Governor of Colonial Virginia* (1932); Julian P. Boyd, "The Sheriff in Colonial North Carolina," *North Carolina Historical Review*, vol. 5 (1928), pp. 151–181; Wilcomb E. Washburn, *The Governor and the Rebel* (1957)*; Robert and B. Katherine Brown, *Virginia, 1705–1786: Democracy or Aristocracy?* (1964); Eugene Sirmans, *Colonial South Carolina. A Political History* (1966); Louis Morton,

Robert Carter of Nomini Hall (1964)*; Aubrey C. Land, *The Dulanys of Maryland* (1955)*; David Mays, *Edmund Pendleton,* 2 vols. (1952); W. W. Abbot, *The Royal Governors of Georgia* (1959).

The Middle Colonies

Lawrence H. Leder, *Robert Livingston, and the Politics of Colonial New York, 1654–1728* (1961); Jerome Reich, *Leisler's Rebellion* (1953); Stanley N. Katz, *Newcastle's New York* (1968); Milton M. Klein, "Democracy and Politics in Colonial New York," *New York History,* vol. 40 (1959), pp. 221–246; William S. Hanna, *Benjamin Franklin and Pennsylvania Politics* (1964); Theodore Thayer, *Pennsylvania Politics and the Growth of Democracy, 1740–1776* (1952).

New England

Oscar Zeichner, *Connecticut's Years of Controversy* (1950); Robert E. Brown, *Middle Class Democracy and the Coming of the Revolution in Massachusetts* (1955)*; David S. Lovejoy, *Rhode Island Politics and the American Revolution* (1958); Mack E. Thompson, "The Ward-Hopkins Controversy and the American Revolution in Rhode Island," *William and Mary Quarterly,* 3d series, vol. 16 (1959), pp. 363–375; John A. Schutz, *William Shirley, King's Governor of Massachusetts* (1961); Jere R. Daniell, "Politics in New Hampshire under Governor Benning Wentworth, 1741–1767," *William and Mary Quarterly,* 3d series, vol. 23 (1966), pp. 76–105; Charles S. Grant, *Democracy in the Frontier Town of Kent* (1961).

British Colonial Administration

Oliver M. Dickerson, *American Colonial Government, 1696– 1765* (1921); Thomas C. Barrow, *Trade and Empire* (1967); Viola F. Barnes, *The Dominion of New England,* (1923); Alison T. Olson, "The British Government and Colonial Union, 1754," *William and Mary Quarterly,* 3d series, vol. 17 (1960), pp. 22– 34; Michael Kammen, *Rope of Sand* (1968); Dora M. Clark,

The Rise of the British Treasury: Colonial Administration in the Eighteenth Century (1960); Michael G. Hall, *Edward Randolph and the American Colonies* (1960).

Freedom of the Press

Leonard Levy, *Freedom of Speech and Press in Early American History* (1960).*

Chapter Five

Sources of American Nationality

In the spring of 1790, almost fifteen years after the American colonies declared their independence, sadness gripped the capital of the young republic. Twenty thousand Philadelphians paid their respects to an individual who had come to symbolize all that was distinctively American. Benjamin Franklin was dead, after a life that spanned the last seventy years of the colonial period. This son of a Boston soapmaker had prospered and won fame both in America and Europe as a statesman, inventor, scientist, and philanthropist. His career provided an example to all enlightened men that genius in the humbly born flowered in a New World which rewarded talent and enterprise. Franklin's life dramatically confirmed a growing conviction that in America man might realize his fullest potential.

Franklin, a self-made man, had little formal schooling. As an apprentice he quarreled with his elder brother, a Boston printer, and moved to Philadelphia. Starting without connections or capital, his talents quickly won both. Franklin was wealthy enough at forty-two to retire. Although isolated from the centers of scientific learning, his experiments in electricity earned the acclaim of Europe's leading intellectuals. Franklin believed in a benevolent God who expected men to do good to others and throughout his life he promoted many schemes for public betterment. Yet Franklin remained always a shrewd politician with a keen instinct for self-advertisement. Fame, money, and position allowed him to instruct others on the path to success, preaching all the godly virtues, such as temperance, silence, order, moderation, chastity, and humility. Franklin attributed success to mastery of them, though his fathering an illegitimate son left questions about his chastity, his ambition and self-promotion raised doubts about his humility, and silence was as unnatural to him as was order.

More revealing than the discrepancies between Franklin's personal ideals and his behavior was the assumption that in America virtue received its just rewards, that man had a real chance to improve himself. America seemed exempt from the infirmities that debased mankind elsewhere. "The Divine Being," Franklin wrote, "seems to have manifested his Approbation . . . by the remarkable Prosperity with which He has been pleased to favor the whole Country."

As his fame spread on two continents Franklin came to symbolize "the new race of men" which some saw springing from the New World, people free from the tyranny, ignorance, poverty, and injustice that hindered mankind's pursuit of happiness elsewhere. Franklin's career suggested that the American social order was an environment uniquely hospitable to the individual's search for fulfillment.

The Social Structure

The ease with which Franklin climbed the colonial social ladder represents a specific instance of a common experience in America. Men were not permanently tied to the social class of their birth. Through their own efforts and luck, they could improve their position. American society, like Europe's, was stratified with elites at the top, but the forms and extent of stratification differed in the New World.

A clear and measurable gradation of status, one that determined men's positions in the social hierarchy, existed in Europe. Those at the top usually possessed wealth, good family, and power. At the apex stood the royal family and the greater nobility, followed by the lesser nobility and landed gentry who ruled over the lower orders. Despite some vertical mobility, law, custom, and limited opportunity fixed most people's station at birth. The sons of peasants expected to remain peasants just as the nobility expected to bequeath their privileged status to their children. Tradition and social custom legitimized this arrangement. So long as men labored at their callings faithfully, there might be peace and order; rebellion brought anarchy. And the great mass of people in the lower strata fatalistically accepted their lot. To be sure, a few aspired to a better life, and even fewer actually achieved an improvement of their condition, but most labored at their tasks "bowed by the weight of centuries."

The first settlers in America intended no great social transformations. But from the beginning American society diverged from Old World patterns. Since few of England's wellborn migrated, the colonies lacked both royalty and nobility, that is, a hereditary aristocracy, to occupy the top of the social order. Nor among the white population was there a large mass of permanently landless folk such as comprised the bulk of English society. The typical white American was a landowner and, even if in possession of a small holding, it was far easier to acquire and keep property than had been the case in England where the numbers of farmers declined in the seventeenth and eighteenth centuries. Without either upper or lower strata comparable to Europe's, the colonies developed a large middle class that included propertied farmers, artisans, merchants, and professionals.

There were colonial elites, however. Neither wealth, nor honor, nor power were equally distributed. But the upper strata in America differed markedly from their peers in Europe. In the first place, the American elite was self-created, not hereditary, recruited from individuals who made the most of opportunities in America. Though some of the elite stemmed from English gentry who migrated armed with advantages, even they had to work hard at securing and maintaining a superior position in the colonies.

Wealth, rather than birth, became the principle source of differentiation in American society, and even inherited property had to be safeguarded. The sons of successful men could not maintain their family's social standing unless they carefully managed their inheritance. The colonial elite, no leisured aristocracy, were usually hard-working estate managers or merchants. Also, a position of dominance brought insecurity with it. Competitive newcomers eagerly seized opportunities, made their way up the social ladder, and pushed to the top. Without strong legal or institutional barriers to hamper them, and since wealth determined eminence, opportunities for rising were readily available.

Southern planters came closest to achieving a way of life resembling the English upper classes. Operating large estates worked by slaves, building impressive, elegantly furnished homes, the Southern gentleman imitated the English squirearchy. Yet for all their cultural pretensions, the planters remained provincials. These speculators in land, producers of tobacco, rice, and indigo, and drivers of slaves had their ranks penetrated often by newcomers. Their inheritance laws (primogeniture and entail) resembled those by which the English aristocracy made certain that the eldest son received and bequeathed the family fortune intact. In America, however, fathers could generally endow their younger sons with land and status making such practices unnecessary or impractical.

Urban elites were even more unstable. In cities and towns trade afforded the principal means to wealth but a merchant's success involved risks. Overseas trade required heavy investments in long voyages and speculation in unstable markets. Such fortunes could be quickly made but they could be lost just as quickly. Equally uncertain were the profits dependent on political favor, such as contracts to supply the British army and navy. Keen competition for these favors meant that a merchant enjoying them one day might lose them in the shifting winds of patronage politics. Nor could those who made money in trade safely withdraw it for reinvestment elsewhere. No corporate bonds or stocks, and few government securities, existed; land speculation was tempting but risky. Yet if he remained in trade the successful merchant exposed himself anew to the uncertainties of business. As a result shrewd newcomers pushed aside older merchants. Thus the roster of leading urban families in the late colonial period differed from those of earlier generations.

Instability similarly affected the professions. With no clear qualifications for becoming a preacher, lawyer, or doctor, few men received formal training except clergymen. Thus no widely accepted professional standards of practice developed. American doctors, observed a well-trained Scottish physician, were "all empyricks, having no knowledge of learning, but what they have acquired by bare experience." Medicine had not yet become a lucrative occupation. Many doctors took "care of a family for the value of a Dutch dollar a year, which makes the practice of physick a mean thing and unworthy of the application of a gentleman." Professional schools, voluntary regulatory associations, and public licensing systems rarely existed. Consequently people had little protection against charlatan doctors or shyster lawyers. As a result the status of these occupations suffered and membership in them did not assure public respect.

Most white Americans, however, were farmers, and this group was also mobile and unstable. Land owners constantly bought and sold property, abandoning a developed farm to establish themselves on fresh lands, investing in mills, cutting timber, operating taverns—always looking for the main chance that meant admission into the elite. A thin and often-breached line separated the aspiring from the established. As a result, European titles designating a person's social status lost their meaning in America. In Connecticut, a traveler noted that his innkeeper used *the title* "Lady" and observed: "No, I cannot tell for what for she is the homeliest piece both as to mien, make, and dress that ever I saw, . . . but it is needless to dispute her right to the title since we know many upon whom it is bestowed who have as little right as she." Confusion in the use of titles revealed ambiguities in the status hierarchy and the difficulty of determining rank. One consequence was, in the words of Gilbert and Sullivan:

> When everyone is somebody,
> Then no one is anybody.

As colonial society matured in the eighteenth century, opportunity for advancement narrowed. In the more densely settled seaboard, the best land passed into private ownership and its value rose accordingly. The sons of large families had difficulty finding attractive sites for farms near their homes. One could always migrate to less developed areas with abundant land. Many did but others hesitated to leave family, friends, and a familiar environment and preferred a dependent status or took up marginal lands. Likewise, those who stayed in the older areas found it harder to penetrate the community's upper strata of well-established families whereas newer settlements had more room at the top.

In the eighteenth century, wealth became increasingly concentrated. In Boston, for instance, the top 15 percent of the taxpayers owned 66 percent of assessed taxable property in 1771 compared to 52 percent in 1687. Similar stratification occurred in a rural community such as Chester county, Pennsylvania. Both areas experienced economic expansion and population growth, which offered the shrewd and enterprising opportunity to accumulate fortunes, whereas the less enterprising or less lucky became tenant farmers, laborers, servants, or seamen. Thus the percentage of those without property but not dependent on others doubled in Boston between 1687 and 1771. At the same time, the relative standing of the moderately well-off, artisans, mechanics, and shopkeepers declined, though their absolute welfare probably improved as the community as a whole became more prosperous.

Foreign travelers in the colonies noticed the absence of the very poor so prevalent in Europe. Though poverty claimed fewer victims in America, the poor were still numerous enough to require public assistance. New York City's poorhouse sheltered 423 paupers in 1772—not many however out of a population of 25,000. Even in the prosperous colonies, there were orphaned children, blind, aged, and handicapped persons in need of public support. And Negroes, free and slave, in the North and South, remained permanently trapped in a degraded and exploited condition. Yet, for most whites, America offered greater opportunity than was available elsewhere.

Religion in the New World

Unexpected circumstances not only altered traditional social relationships, they also transformed established religious forms. In the seventeenth century no man could publicly reject religion. The Church helped the state maintain order, giving aid considered essential to the governing process. Until the Protestant Reformation shattered the religious monopoly of Catholicism, Europeans shared a single faith, embodied in one established church. People were born into the Church, accepted its doctrines, rituals, and discipline, and provided for its material support. In return, the Church offered to help men find salvation.

Even after Luther and Calvin broke with Rome, people remained convinced that their church—whether Lutheran, Presbyterian, Congregationalist, or Catholic—embodied the true faith. Religious error, or heresy, must be checked. Heretics sinned against their own souls by denying spiritual truth, and they endangered the souls of others. This obliged the state and the church to repress dissent as a threat to all men and to the peace of the community.

Both Massachusetts and Virginia acted on these principles when they established state churches, one Calvinist, the other Anglican. Massachusetts zealously suppressed heresy, exiling Roger Williams and Anne Hutchinson, and executing several Quakers who would not flee. Yet initial denials of religious freedom, though in keeping with accepted European practice, collapsed in the face of pressures that in the eighteenth century produced a gradual victory for the still novel principle of toleration.

Toleration spread because religious persecution proved impractical. New settlements in need of labor could ill afford to turn away immigrants who worshiped differently. Profit-hungry trading companies and proprietors discovered that it made more sense to welcome the able-bodied whatever their beliefs. But New England stood in no such need since the Puritan colonies received large numbers of coreligionists fleeing from persecution in England. Outside the closely knit townships of New England, settlements were dispersed and often without churches to enforce uniformity. Should a colony attempt to suppress dissent, those persecuted could easily find refuge elsewhere in other more tolerant communities. The wilderness always offered an escape. England depended on private enterprise to establish colonies in America, and paid little attention to the colonizing group's religious inclinations. This enabled Catholics in Maryland and Puritans in New England to worship as they pleased despite the fact that in England tolerance of nonconforming Protestants did not come until after 1689.

Officially the Church of England was the established church in Britain, and other denominations, though tolerated, suffered disabilities. Anglicanism was likewise established in Virginia, Maryland, the Carolinas, and Georgia. But elsewhere it existed in competition with other churches, and in New England at the sufferance of the Congregationalist establishment. For these reasons religious diversity came to America very early, and the passage of time strengthened it. Thus, the crown unintentionally promoted religious variation.

New sources of immigration in the eighteenth century contributed to the diversity as Scotch-Irish Presbyterians, English Quakers, German Lutherans, and Pietist sects poured into the colonies. At the same time that the religious character of the Americans became more varied, new colonies appeared which from the beginning treated all religions alike, favoring none with state support. Pennsylvania was the most notable haven for dissenters but they also found a tolerant spirit in New Jersey and New York.

Pennsylvania tolerance rested on more than expediency. Quakers, like other Pietists, and like Roger Williams, held that religious belief was a private matter between man and God; the state therefore had no right to intrude. Toleration was necessary so that each person could commune freely with God. They insisted that the state respect man's conscience. Quakers and other Pietists thus added the force of principle to the lure of expediency that had strengthened the idea of toleration.

As toleration spread, so did diversity in belief. And as many Americans became more concerned with their lives in this world than the next, it became harder for the state to persecute dissent. Ultimately, the sheer number of competing denominations —Congregationalists, Anglicans, Presbyterians, Baptists, Quakers, Lutherans, German and Dutch Reformed, to mention only the leading groups—prevented any one from enjoying a monopoly. Catholics, however, feared and hated by all Protestant denominations were subject to discrimination.

An even more radical change than the spread of toleration was a steady erosion in the ties between church and state. Some colonies such as Pennsylvania and Rhode Island did not establish churches. Contrary to orthodox expectations, these communities remained peaceful and prosperous. Elsewhere religious establishments failed to achieve or maintain the influence of European state churches. In the South, dissenters often outnumbered Anglicans and the Church of England was the established church in name only. Establishments remained strongest in New England because of weaker pressures from dissenting sects. Yet even in the Puritan colonies, growing numbers of Anglicans, Quakers, and Baptists forced the acceptance of change. They refused to contribute to the Congregational churches. The Congregationalists preserved establishment by grudgingly permitting dissenters to allocate their church taxes for support of their own sects. Thus Massachusetts in the eighteenth century acquired multiple establishments.

The separation of church and state in some colonies, and the weakening of traditional ties between the two elsewhere, were the roots of an American tradition according to which religious concerns are private matters. Already in the colonial period, a new mode of organizing religious life—denomination-alism—began to replace the idea of established churches. In the absence of state support, churches became voluntary associations, enjoying legal equality with all other sects. Lacking state compulsion to enforce membership and provide financial support, denominations depended on lay support and had to recruit adherents. Nevertheless, the absence of state aid had advantages. In order to grow, denominations had to serve public needs, involve citizens actively in their affairs, and compete for members. The voluntary principle conformed to the Pietist belief that exalted personal religious experiences over formal belief and ritual. Even the established Anglican church in the South reflected the powerful forces transforming the churches in America. Theoretically controlled by the Bishop of London, Anglican churches fell under the control of prominent laymen in the parish and had to rely on voluntary support.

The power of the voluntary principle in nurturing a vigorous religious life became strikingly clear in the 1730s when an upheaval called the Great Awakening took place. During the final forty years of the colonial period, Americans experienced recurrent religious revivals that reached a peak in the 1740s but reappeared for over a century. Revivals were intense, emotional reawakenings among people racked with the guilt of sin, the fear of damnation, and the desire for rebirth. Revivalism was also a technique for saving souls by shaking men out of their indifference and filling the hearts of sinners with terror. Yet they also offered a chance for salvation. The message of the Awakening spread in the colonies through the powerful oratory of preachers, such as Jonathan Edwards of Massachusetts, and the English revivalist George Whitefield. The signs of sin, they proclaimed, were everywhere: Sabbath breaking, abstention from church services, intemperance, a love for luxury, and, of course, loose morals.

During the second half of the seventeenth century, New England ministers endlessly noted and lamented a decline of piety since the days of the founding generation. Yet denunciations, however vivid or powerful, could not hold back change. The children of the Calvinist first settlers, born in America, had not shared the experiences of the founders. Their lives and aspirations were defined, not by the covenant with God, but by the prospects of settling a new land. The Puritan creed sanctioned hard work and perseverance, and urged men to pursue their callings energetically; but later generations found it increasingly difficult to subordinate worldly ambitions to spiritual duties. Life in the New World demonstrated that on earth men were not prisoners of a prearranged fate. They possessed a free will, and the ability to advance their earthly fortunes. Deviation from the original mission of the first settlers generated tension and guilt because although later generations no longer entirely believed in the ancient faith, they could not totally abandon their spiritual heritage. Instead, men sought ways of purging their guilt.

New Englanders attempted to halt the decline in piety by loosening church membership standards. Before 1648 only children of those who had experienced conversion, the "Saints," were baptized into the church. Subsequently children of the unconverted could become halfway members, if they led outwardly pious lives. Eventually, most congregations abolished the distinction between halfway and full members, no longer requiring a specific conversion experience for admission.

In the 1690s, alarm spread through Massachusetts when several hysterical teen-age girls in Salem convinced authorities that they were the victims of witchcraft. The craze led to the arrest of over 400 alleged witches and warlocks and the execution of twenty persons. Following four months of frenzy the colony regained its senses and the imprisonments and executions stopped. Though belief in witchcraft was widespread throughout the Western world, the outbreak in Massachusetts at that time provided a way to acknowledge that sin flourished, and that the agents of the devil lurked about everywhere, even among close neighbors. By identifying and punishing the

witches, the preachers with the state's aid, felt they were battling spiritual decline. By destroying the "forces of evil," the
Puritan clergy briefly resumed the great power they had enjoyed
during the founding generation.

But faith continued to decline. Conversions were fewer,
church attendance dropped, and in New England and elsewhere
people became increasingly absorbed in this world, not the next.
As men mastered their environment, the supernatural concerned
them less. Man, rather than God, became the center of their
universe.

This secularization of outlook occurred slowly and unevenly.
People, only a few generations removed from a time when salvation was regarded as man's first concern, did not easily shake
off centuries of belief. From time to time they encountered ill-
fortune. When affairs did not go as they hoped or intended,
they doubted their capacities and found refuge in the supernatural. The revival offered hope. By confession and reliance
on God's mercy, one might be saved. Though the ministers
preached that only God could save, they also demanded that
their listeners repent and actively seek forgiveness. In an extraordinary intellectual and emotional enterprise, Jonathan Edwards, among others, attempted to update Calvinist theology
and the forms of Christian worship to reverse the decline of
faith and piety.

The religious revival was a communal experience. People
gathered at the riversides and in the public squares in throngs,
praying, singing, and writhing together. For a moment they
found fellowship among other sinners.

The revival also offered temporary release from the pressures of everyday existence, as men joined with their neighbors,
high and low, in a common demonstration of piety and community solidarity. Paradoxically, the increased religiosity of the
revivals further weakened the hold of orthodox religion. Benevolence toward fellowmen became more important than doctrines
or rituals. And since every man could be saved, this equality of
spiritual opportunity matched the abundance of worldly oppor-

tunity in America. Self-confidence about earthly matters, bred self-confidence about salvation. A century earlier orthodox Puritans had preached that salvation came only through selection by a sovereign and unpredictable God. The revival thus adjusted religious life to the American experience.

The Great Awakening had far-reaching consequences. Stress on ethical behavior as a sign of conversion gave impetus to a broad range of humanitarian concerns for the condition of the drunkard, the slave, and the helpless. The Awakening further weakened the hold of established churches, dividing many congregations. Some ministers resented the intrusion of itinerant preachers more gifted than they at exhorting crowds, and many Christians rejected the appeal to emotions which provoked the crowd to convulsions and wild shouting. As churches divided into pro- and anti-revival factions, the minority often withdrew to form new congregations. In this way dozens of new churches appeared in New England, some remaining Congregationalists, others becoming Baptist.

The inclination of antirevivalists to use state power to curb revivalism, and especially itinerant preachers, increased hostility to state control over spiritual affairs. Moreover, by further fragmenting the structure of American Christianity, by insisting that the churches must actively seek out sinners, and by involving people in a Christian crusade, the Great Awakening strengthened already existing tendencies toward denominationalism.

Yet its most important function was to relieve men temporarily of the guilt of secularism, the subordination of spiritual values to worldly ones. Through confession and rebirth, people found momentary relief and gained new psychological strength to resume the struggle for earthly happiness. The revival thus offered a continuing opportunity for intense but occasional spirituality that did not reverse the trend toward secularization.

By the end of the colonial period a distinctive American pattern of religious life had emerged, based on tolerance, church-state separation, and denominationalism. The particular needs of religion in the wilderness and the growing proliferation of sects helped to shape a distinctively American culture whose characteristics are further revealed by developments in education and science.

Education in a New World

Universal literacy and free public schooling for all did not arrive until the nineteenth century. In Europe and in the American colonies of the seventeenth and eighteenth centuries the upper classes enjoyed the luxury of formal education. Most children learned the skills they would need in life, acquired the values and attitudes of the adult world, and were taught to read by a literate relative or neighbor. Many remained illiterate.

The family and the church were the principal instruments by which society transmitted its standards of behavior from one generation to the next. The children of peasants learned how to work at home and in the fields. Those who became artisans learned their trade as apprentices in the households and shops of master craftsmen. Schooling remained the preserve of the more fortunate members of society, those expected to provide leadership. In English preparatory schools young men trained for the professions. Those becoming lawyers, doctors, or merchants received further training from established members of the professions; others, especially aspiring clergymen, enrolled at the universities of Oxford and Cambridge. Since most occupations did not require formal education, and few needed the skills it developed, conditions which led to the democratization of educational opportunity did not then exist.

The situation in the colonies was similar, though the American environment subtly altered the character of education there. Settlers established schools and colleges but English patterns were not entirely appropriate to colonial conditions. The first generation of settlers, conscious that they shared an untamed wilderness with Indian tribes, considered uncivilized, did not stray far from European cultural norms. Colonists feared that the wilderness would engulf them, unless some of them were literate and trained in the professions. The pressure to establish schools was greatest in the Puritan colonies, especially Massachusetts. In the Bay colony, government forcefully attempted to achieve communal goals through state action. In 1642 the legislature required all towns with fifty families or more to maintain an elementary school and towns with 100 families had to establish a grammar school as well. Support for the schools became the responsibility of each town under threat of fines for noncompliance.

The hopes of the first generation went unfulfilled. Later generations, especially those living in the country, were reluctant to support schools, preferring instead to pay fines for noncompliance. As religious fervor declined, one of the principal impulses spurring the creation of public schools weakened. Furnishing a steady supply of ministers and teaching people to read the Bible became less urgent. In other colonies, where the initial religious impulses had been weaker and where formally educated leaders were more rare, government was even less disposed to establish schools and education became largely a voluntary effort. Moreover, the low density of population, an inclination to invest capital in farms and businesses rather than in social services, created additional obstacles. The well-to-do could hire tutors or pay fees at private schools; others did not need schooling to prosper.

Higher education received greater support. Massachusetts founded Harvard College in 1636, but until the end of the seventeenth century Harvard stood alone. Those who did not attend the Puritan college, had to journey to England, an alternative preferred by the sons of southern planters. Eventually, however, sufficient pressure developed in Virginia to establish the College of William and Mary (1693) and fresh needs in New England led to the founding of Yale in 1701. After 1745 the number of colleges grew rapidly. By the end of the colonial period ten institutions of higher learning existed, compared with only two in England, although the American colleges could not yet be compared with the universities of Oxford and Cambridge.

The growth of colleges resulted from both sectarian and secular pressures. Over 100 college graduates arrived in New

England during the Great Migration (1630–1640), many of them ministers. Thus from the beginning Massachusetts possessed educated leaders, lay and secular. To assure a constant supply of trained clergy and officials, Puritans established educational institutions that would transmit and perpetuate their values. Other groups followed: Anglicans created William and Mary, Baptists founded Brown, and Presbyterians established Princeton.

The weakening of the ties between church and state, and the acceptance of the voluntary principle in religious life, intensified the pressures for denominationally sponsored colleges. More than any other institution, the church became the center of communal life and a source of group identity. People thought of themselves as Massachusetts Congregationalists, Virginia Anglicans, or Pennsylvania Quakers. Sects which had to compete with one another for members, and which could not rely on state support, made special efforts to perpetuate their group in a religiously open society. The college became a vital foundation of denominational survival and growth.

Though sectarian energies established the colleges, they served more than the needs of the controlling denomination. The colonial colleges trained students in the liberal arts and sciences, preparing them for a variety of callings, not solely the ministry. In the eighteenth century the percentage of graduates who became ministers declined as men found more rewarding careers in trade, government, law, and medicine.

While the colleges served the needs of sectarians, they also represented self-conscious efforts to maintain English cultural standards in America and to furnish society with an educated leadership that would maintain order. Without the existence of Harvard, a commencement orator warned in the 1670s, "The ruling class would have been subjected to mechanics, cobblers, and tailors; we would have no rights, honors or magisterial ordinances worthy of preservation, but plebiscites, appeals to base passions, and revolutionary rumblings." College-educated leaders, in turn, received training that fitted them for the responsibilities of their position in society, helping to preserve them from the "vice of a certain class, by giving them easy access to more refined pleasure and inspiring the mind with an abhorrence of low riot and contempt for brutal conversation." At least that was the theory.

The increasingly secular mission of the college gained strength in the eighteenth century. Though diverse sects established such new institutions as Columbia and Princeton, it was necessary to enlist support from other groups in order to obtain charters of incorporation from the legislatures. Conditions for such support were the admission of students regardless of creed, and instruction that did not offend the sectarian sensibilities of the several groups that backed and attended the college. Colleges increasingly came to serve society's needs, rather than that of a single sect. The growing tendency among those entering college in the late colonial period to seek nonministerial careers further weakened denominationalism in higher education. College curricula began to reflect an interest in science and modern languages as well as the traditional emphasis on the classics, philosophy, and theology.

Despite the proliferation of colleges in America, and the vast labor invested in them, they achieved their original aims only partially. In England higher education remained a monopoly of the established church but in America the variety of sects prevented one group from dominating higher education. American colleges were less under the sway of the church, but they became more dependent upon community support, especially the newer institutions which lacked the extensive endowments of European universities. Whereas the faculties controlled European universities, American colleges fell into the hands of the trustees who represented the supporting community.

Thomas Jefferson and John Adams were college graduates, but Benjamin Franklin and George Washington were not. Because the American social order was open, talent, hard work, and genius counted for more and the possession of a college degree for less than in England. A college education was not so valuable in the competition for wealth and position as it later became; it was not yet a professional "union card."

Toward an American Culture

The Americans, a French visitor observed near the end of the colonial period were "the western pilgrims . . . carrying along with them the great mass of arts, sciences, vigour, and industry which began long since in the east; they will finish the great circle." In less than two centuries, as British colonial subjects, the Americans developed a style of life that distinguished them from the rest of mankind. The attitudes and institutions people brought to America from Europe changed as settlers adapted themselves to a new environment. America appeared different from Europe because its people were generally more prosperous, freer to govern themselves, to worship as they pleased, and advance their individual position in society. Above all, the American was optimistic, confident of his power to control his destiny and reap earthly rewards.

Though the colonists transformed the nature of the state, the church, and the social structure, they took only halting steps in the development of a native culture that expressed American imagination in the arts and sciences. From the beginning, the workings of nature aroused colonial curiosity. Scientific inquiry reflected American expansive opportunities and circumstances. Americans showed most interest in natural history. The wilderness was full of unfamiliar and unclassified specimens which colonists supplied European scientists. Those with scientific curiosity could make distinctive contributions in a field that required relatively little professional training, whereas the physical sciences demanded greater technical knowledge.

Ben Franklin, however, made important contributions to the understanding of electricity precisely because little was known about it in Europe. As an amateur, out of touch with Europe's learned world, Franklin could let his scientific imagination freely wander along original paths which those operating within the conventional boundaries of European scientific opinion did not follow. Moreover, Franklin's mind had a practical bent. Though his investigations originated in curiosity about the natural world, he also sought to make scientific knowledge useful.

Similarly, American medicine lacked professionalization at a time when the healing arts were still rudimentary. European doctors had little understanding of the causes and cure of disease. Learning their trades as apprentices, rather than through formal schooling, American doctors were less prone to perpetuate the mistaken theories that dominated much of European medicine. They were also more inclined to rely on natural cures and treatments developed from practical experience. Thus the first large-scale use of inoculation against smallpox occurred in Boston because professional medical opinion, which was skeptical, was not powerful enough to block the experiment. Subsequently the success of inoculation encouraged its spread throughout Europe.

The arts in America, like science, developed far from the centers of cultural life. The first American painters lacked the technical skills possessed by European artists. Their portraits, anything but sophisticated, were still simple and realistic renderings of their subjects. As the colonies matured, eighteenth century painters acquired more skill and some American patrons demanded portraits more like those which flattered Europe's highborn. Artists, in imitating English styles, departed from the earlier colonial preference for pictures that were direct and honest.

The same ambivalence marked colonial architecture. Many styles influenced colonial buildings, reflecting the cultural diversity of the times. German, Dutch, and English, Anglicans and Puritans, erected the type of structures with which they were familiar. As the colonies prospered, public buildings and private residences became more costly and elaborate. American elites imitated the Georgian style favored by eighteenth century English leaders. This was a pretentious, highly derivative and imitative architectural style. At the same time a distinctively American building form developed. The American colonial cottage, the home of the middle classes, was a simple yet graceful rectangular dwelling, notable for its light frame construction, its use of wood which in Europe was scarce, and its numerous windows.

For all their interest in the arts and sciences, the life of the mind and the play of the imagination remained remote from the center of colonial concern. These isolated provincials had to establish a society far from the centers of learning and culture. Americans concentrated on taming the wilderness and advancing their individual fortunes. Someday, they would paint pictures, write stories, and erect buildings at which others would marvel. But they would first have to create an American nation.

Document: A British Visitor to the Colonies, 1759–1760
Reverend Andrew Burnaby's Travel Notes

Andrew Burnaby was born in 1734, the son of a prosperous Anglican minister. He studied at Cambridge University and like his father became an Anglican clergyman, the Vicar of Greenwich. He traveled in the American colonies in 1759–1760 and again in 1762–1767 and published his impressions in 1775 which were soon translated into French and German. Burnaby was one of a growing number of European visitors curious about what was happening in the colonies. Unlike many French travelers, Burnaby was ambivalent toward the colonies as is suggested by his contrasting pictures of Virginia and Pennsylvania reprinted below. Though he visited the colonies on the eve of the events leading to the American Revolution, Burnaby, like most colonists, had no inkling of the troubles ahead and did not perceive, as most Americans did not, the extent to which the colonists were united by a common colonial experience. That perception grew under the stress of the revolutionary crisis.

Source: Andrew Burnaby, *Andrew Burnaby's Travels Through North America 1759–1760* (New York, 1904), pp. 53–59, 91–99, 153–155.

. . . From what has been said of this colony [Virginia], it will not be difficult to form an idea of the character[1] of its inhabitants. The climate and external appearance of the country conspire to make them indolent, easy, and good natured; extremely fond of society, and much given to convivial pleasures. In consequence of this, they seldom show any spirit of enterprise, or expose themselves willingly to fatigue. Their authority over their slaves renders them vain and imperious, and entire strangers to that elegance of sentiment, which is so peculiarly characteristic of refined and polished nations. Their ignorance of mankind and of learning, exposes them to many errors and prejudices, especially in regard to Indians and negroes, whom they scarcely consider as of the human species; so that it is almost impossible, in cases of violence, or even murder, committed upon those unhappy people by any of the planters, to have the delinquents brought to justice: for either the grand jury refuse to find the bill, or the petit jury bring in their verdict, not guilty.

The display of a character thus constituted, will naturally be in acts of extravagance, ostentation, and a disregard of economy; it is not extraordinary therefore, that the Virginians outrun their incomes; and that having involved themselves in difficulties, they are frequently tempted to raise money by bills of exchange, which they know will be returned protested, with 10 percent interest.

The public or political character of the Virginians corresponds with their private one: they are haughty and jealous of

[1] General characteristics are always liable to many exceptions. In Virginia, I have had the pleasure to know several gentlemen adorned with many virtues and accomplishments, to whom the following description is by no means applicable. Amongst others, I cannot resist the inclination of mentioning George Wythe, Esquire, who, to a perfect knowledge of the Greek language, which was taught him by his mother in the back woods, and of the ancient, particularly the Platonic philosophy, had joined such a profound reverence for the Supreme Being, such respect for the divine laws, such philanthropy for mankind, such simplicity of manners, and such inflexible rectitude and integrity of principle, as would have dignified a Roman senator, even in the most virtuous times of the republic. This gentleman is, I believe, still living.

their liberties, impatient of restraint, and can scarcely bear the thought of being controlled by any superior power. Many of them consider the colonies as independent states, not connected with Great Britain, otherwise than by having the same common king, and being bound to her by natural affection. There are but few of them that have a turn for business, and even those are by no means expert at it. I have known them, upon a very urgent occasion, vote the relief of a garrison, without once considering whether the thing was practicable, when it was most evidently and demonstrably otherwise. In matters of commerce they are ignorant of the necessary principles that must prevail between a colony and the mother country; they think it a hardship not to have an unlimited trade to every part of the world. They consider the duties upon their staple as injurious only to themselves; and it is utterly impossible to persuade them that they affect the consumer also. However, to do them justice, the same spirit of generosity prevails here which does in their private character; they never refuse any necessary supplies for the support of government when called upon, and are a generous and loyal people.

The women are, generally speaking, handsome, though not to be compared with our fair countrywomen in England. They have but few advantages, and consequently are seldom accomplished; this makes them reserved, and unequal to any interesting or refined conversation. They are immoderately fond of dancing, and indeed it is almost the only amusement they partake of: but even in this they discover want of taste and elegance, and seldom appear with that gracefulness and ease, which these movements are calculated to display. Towards the close of an evening, when the company are pretty well tired with country dances, it is usual to dance jigs; a practice originally borrowed, I am informed, from the negroes. These dances are without method or regularity: a gentleman and lady stand up, and dance about the room, one of them retiring, the other pursuing, then perhaps meeting, in an irregular fantastical manner. After some time, another lady gets up, and then the first lady must sit down, she being, as they term it, cut out: the second lady acts the same part which the first did, till somebody cuts her out. The gentlemen perform in the same manner. The Virginian ladies, excepting these amusements, and now and then going upon a party of pleasure into the woods to partake of a barbecue, chiefly spend their time in sewing and taking care of their families: they seldom read, or endeavour to improve their minds; however, they are in general good housewives; and though they have not, I think, quite so much tenderness and sensibility as the English ladies, yet they make as good wives, and as good mothers, as any in the world.

It is hard to determine whether this colony can be called flourishing, or not; because though it produces great quantities of tobacco and grain, yet there seem to be very few improvements carrying on in it. Great part of Virginia is a wilderness, and as many of the gentlemen are in possession of immense tracts of land, it is likely to continue so. A spirit of enterprise is by no means the turn of the colony, and therefore few attempts have been made to force a trade; which I think might easily be done, both to the West Indies and the Ohio. They have every thing necessary for such an undertaking; viz. lumber, provisions, grain, and every other commodity, which the other colonies, that subsist and grow rich by these means, make use of for exports; but, instead of this, they have only a trifling communication with the West Indies; and as to the Ohio, they have suffered themselves, notwithstanding the superior advantages they might enjoy from having a water carriage almost to the Youghiogheny, to neglect this valuable branch of commerce; while the industrious Pennsylvanians seize every opportunity, and struggle with innumerable difficulties to secure it to themselves. The Virginians are content if they can but live from day to day; they confine themselves almost entirely to the cultivation of tobacco; and if they have but enough of this to pay their merchants in London, and to provide for their pleasures, they are satisfied, and desire nothing more. Some few, indeed, have been rather more enterprising, and have endeavoured to improve their estates by raising indigo, and other schemes: but whether it has been owing to the climate, to their inexperience in these matters, or their want of perseverance, I am unable to determine. . . .

Can the mind have a greater pleasure than in contemplating the rise and progress of cities and kingdoms? Than in perceiving a rich and opulent state arising out of a small settlement or colony? This pleasure every one must feel who considers Pennsylvania. This wonderful province is situated between the 40th and 43d degree of north latitude, and about 76 degrees west longitude from London, in a healthy and delightful climate, amidst all the advantages that nature can bestow. The soil is extremely strong and fertile, and produces spontaneously an infinite variety of trees, flowers, fruits, and plants of different sorts. The mountains are enriched with ore, and the rivers with fish: some of these are so stately as not to be beheld without admiration: the Delaware is navigable for large vessels as far as the falls, 180 miles distant from the sea, and 120 from the bay. At the mouth it is more than three miles broad, and above one at Philadelphia. The navigation is obstructed in the winter, for about six weeks, by the severity of the frost; but, at other times, it is bold and open. The Schuylkill, though not navigable for any great space, is exceedingly romantic, and affords the most delightful retirements.

Cultivation (comparatively speaking) is carried to a high degree of perfection; and Pennsylvania produces not only great plenty, but also great variety of grain; it yields likewise flax-seed, hemp, cattle of different kinds, and various other articles.[2]

---

[2] In the southern colonies cultivation is in a very low state. The common process of it is, first to cut off the trees two or three feet above ground, in order to let in the sun and air, leaving the stumps to decay and rot, which they do in a few years. After this they dig and plant, and continue to work the same field, year after year, without ever manuring it, till it is quite spent. They then enter upon a fresh piece of ground, allowing this a respite of about twenty years to recover itself; during which time it becomes beautifully covered with Virginian pines; the seeds of that tree, which are exceedingly small, and, when the cones open, are wafted through the air in great abundance, sowing themselves in every vacant spot of neglected ground.

It is divided into eight counties, and contains many large and populous towns: Carlisle, Lancaster, and Germantown, consist each of near five hundred houses; there are several others which have from one or two hundred.

The number of inhabitants is supposed to be between four and five hundred thousand, a fifth of which are Quakers; there are very few negroes or slaves.

The trade of Pennsylvania is surprisingly extensive, carried on to Great Britain, the West Indies, every part of North America, the Madeiras, Lisbon, Cadiz, Holland, Africa, the Spanish Main, and several other places; exclusive of what is illicitly carried on to Cape François, and Monte Christo. Their exports are provisions of all kinds, lumber, hemp, flax, flax-seed, iron, furs, and deer-skins. Their imports, English manufactures, with the superfluities and luxuries of life. By their flag-of-truce trade, they also get sugar, which they refine and send to Europe.

Their manufactures are very considerable. The Germantown thread-stockings are in high estimation; and the year before last, I have been credibly informed, there were manufactured in that town alone above 60,000 dozen pair. Their common retail price is a dollar per pair.

The Irish settlers make very good linens: some woolens have also been fabricated, but not, I believe, to any amount. There are several other manufactures, viz. of beaver hats, which are superior in goodness to any in Europe, of cordage, linseed-oil, starch, myrtle-wax and spermaceti candles, soap, earthen ware, and other commodities.

The government of this province is a proprietary one. The legislature is lodged in the hands of a governor, appointed (with the king's approbation) by the proprietor; and a house of representatives elected by the people, consisting of thirty-seven members. These are of various religious persuasions; for by the charter of privileges which Mr. Penn granted to the settlers in Pennsylvania, no person who believed in God could be molested in his calling or profession; and any one who believed in Jesus Christ might enjoy the first post under the government. The crown has reserved to itself a power of repealing any law, which may interfere with the prerogative, or be contrary to the laws of Great Britain. . . .

As to religion, there is none properly established; but Protestants of all denominations, Papists, Jews, and all other sects whatsoever, are universally tolerated. There are twelve clergymen of the Church of England, who are sent by the Society for the Propagation of the Gospel, and are allowed annually 50 l. each, besides what they get from subscriptions and surplice fees. Some few of these are itinerant missionaries, and have no fixed residence, but travel from place to place, as occasion requires, upon the frontiers. They are under the jurisdiction of the bishop of London.

Arts and sciences are yet in their infancy. There are some few persons who have discovered a taste for music and painting; and philosophy seems not only to have made a considerable progress already, but to be daily gaining ground. The library society is an excellent institution for propagating a taste for literature; and the college well calculated to form and cultivate it. This last institution is erected upon an admirable plan, and is by far the best school for learning throughout America. It has been chiefly raised by contributions; and its present fund is about 10,000 l. Pennsylvania money. An account of it may be seen in Dr. Smith's (the president's) Discourses. The Quakers also have an academy for instructing their youth in classical learning, and practical mathematics: there are three teachers, and about seventy boys in it. Besides these, there are several schools in the province for the Dutch and other foreign children; and a considerable one is going to be erected at Germantown.

The Pennsylvanians, as to character, are a frugal and industrious people: not remarkably courteous and hospitable to strangers, unless particularly recommended to them; but rather, like the denizens of most commercial cities, the reverse. They are great republicans, and have fallen into the same errors in their ideas of independency as most of the other colonies have. They are by far the most enterprising people upon the continent.

As they consist of several nations, and talk several languages, they are aliens in some respect to Great Britain: nor can it be expected that they should have the same filial attachment to her which her own immediate offspring have. However, they are quiet, and concern themselves but little, except about getting money. The women are exceedingly handsome and polite; they are naturally sprightly and fond of pleasure; and, upon the whole, are much more agreeable and accomplished than the men. Since their intercourse with the English officers, they are greatly improved; and, without flattery, many of them would not make bad figures even in the first assemblies in Europe. Their amusements are chiefly, dancing in the winter; and, in the summer, forming parties of pleasure upon the Schuylkill, and in the country. There is a society of sixteen ladies, and as many gentlemen, called the fishing company, who meet once a fortnight upon the Schuylkill. They have a very pleasant room erected in a romantic situation upon the banks of that river, where they generally dine and drink tea. There are several pretty walks about it, and some wild and rugged rocks, which, together with the water and fine groves that adorn the banks, form a most beautiful and picturesque scene. There are boats and fishing tackle of all sorts, and the company divert themselves with walking, fishing, going up the water, dancing, singing, conversing, or just as they please. The ladies wear an uniform, and appear with great ease and advantage from the neatness and simplicity of it. The first and most distinguished people of the colony are of this society; and it is very advantageous to a stranger to be introduced to it, as he hereby gets acquainted with the best and most respectable company in Philadelphia. In the winter, when there is snow upon the ground, it is usual to make what they call sleighing parties, or to go upon it in sledges; but as this is a practice well known in Europe, it is needless to describe it.

The present state of Pennsylvania is undoubtedly very flourishing. The country is well cultivated, and there are not less than 9,000 wagons employed in it, in different services. Till this war they were exempt from taxes; and it was not without difficulty that the Quakers were prevailed upon to grant any supplies for the defence of the frontiers, though exposed to the most horrid cruelties: it was not from principle, say their enemies, that they refused it, but from interest; for as they were the first settlers, they chiefly occupy the interior and lower parts of the province, and are not exposed to incursions. At length, however, compelled by clamour and public discontent, they were obliged to pass a supply bill for 100,000 l. to raise five and twenty hundred men; and these they have kept up ever since; they afterward passed a militia bill, but it was such an one as answered no good purpose. The Quakers have much the greatest influence in the assembly, and are supported there by the Dutch and Germans, who are as adverse to taxes as themselves. Their power, however, at present seems rather on the decline; which is the reason, as the opposite party pretend, that they stir upon all occasions as much confusion as possible, from that trite maxim in politics, *divide et impera.* They have quarrelled with the proprietors upon several occasions, whether altogether justly or not, I will not pretend to say; it is certain, however, that the determinations at home have been sometimes in their favour. The late subjects of their disputes have been chiefly these:

First, Whether the proprietary lands ought to be taxed? This has been determined at home in the affirmative.

Secondly, Whether the proprietor ought to have any choice or approbation of the assessors?

Thirdly, Whether he ought to give his governor instructions? And,

Lastly, Whether the judges of his appointment ought to be during pleasure, or *quamdiu se bene gesserint* [on good behavior]? These three last are still undecided. . . .

Having travelled over so large a tract of this vast continent, before I bid a final farewell to it, I must beg the reader's indulgence, while I stop for a moment, and as it were from the top of a high eminence, take one general retrospective look at the whole. An idea, strange as it is visionary, has entered into the minds of the generality of mankind, that empire is travelling westward; and every one is looking forward with eager and impatient expectation to that destined moment when America is to give law to the rest of the world. But if ever an idea was illusory and fallacious, I am fully persuaded, that this will be so.

America is formed for happiness, but not for empire: in a course of 1,200 miles I did not see a single object that solicited charity; but I saw insuperable causes of weakness, which will necessarily prevent its being a potent state.

Our colonies may be distinguished into the southern and northern, separated from each other by the Susquehanna and that imaginary line which divides Maryland from Pennsylvania.

The southern colonies have so many inherent causes of weakness, that they never can possess any real strength. The climate operates very powerfully upon them, and renders them indolent, inactive, and unenterprising; this is visible in every line of their character. I myself have been a spectator, and it is not an uncommon sight, of a man in the vigour of life, lying upon a couch, and a female slave standing over him, wafting off the flies, and fanning him, while he took his repose.

The southern colonies (Maryland, which is the smallest and most inconsiderable, alone excepted) will never be thickly seated: for as they are not confined within determinate limits, but extend to the westward indefinitely, men, sooner than apply to laborious occupations, occupations militating with their dispositions, and generally considered too as the inheritance and badge of slavery, will gradually retire westward, and settle upon fresh lands, which are said also to be more fertile; where, by the servitude of a negro or two, they may enjoy all the satisfaction of an easy and indolent independency: hence the lands upon the coast will of course remain thin of inhabitants.

The mode of cultivation by slavery, is another insurmountable cause of weakness. The number of negroes in the southern colonies is upon the whole nearly equal, if not superior, to that of the white men; and they propagate and increase even faster. Their condition is truly pitiable; their labour excessively hard, their diet poor and scanty, their treatment cruel and oppressive: they cannot therefore but be a subject of terror to those who so inhumanly tyrannize over them.

The Indians near the frontiers are a still further formidable cause of subjection. The southern Indians are numerous, and are governed by a sounder policy than formerly: experience has taught them wisdom. They never make war with the colonists without carrying terror and devastation along with them. They sometimes break up entire counties together. Such is the state of the southern colonies.

The northern colonies are of stronger stamina, but they have other difficulties and disadvantages to struggle with, not less arduous, or more easy to be surmounted, than what have been already mentioned. Their limits being defined, they will undoubtedly become exceedingly populous: for though men will readily retire back towards the frontiers of their own colony, yet they will not so easily be induced to settle beyond them, where different laws and polities prevail; and where, in short, they are a different people: but in proportion to want of territory, if we consider the proposition in a general and abstract light, will be want of power. But the northern colonies have still more positive and real disadvantages to contend with. They are composed of people of different nations, different manners, different religions, and different languages. They have a mutual jealousy of each other, fomented by considerations of interest, power, and ascendancy. Religious zeal, too, like a smothered fire, is secretly burning in the hearts of the different sectaries that inhabit them, and were it not restrained by laws and superior authority, would soon burst out into a flame of universal persecution. Even the peaceable Quakers struggle hard for pre-eminence, and evince in a very striking manner that the passions of mankind are much stronger than any principles of religion.

The colonies, therefore, separately considered, are internally weak; but it may be supposed, that, by an union or coalition, they would become strong and formidable: but an union seems almost impossible: one founded in dominion or power is morally so: for, were not England to interfere, the colonies themselves so well understand the policy of preserving a balance, that, I think, they would not be idle spectators, were any one of them to endeavour to subjugate its next neighbour. Indeed, it appears to me a very doubtful point, even supposing all the colonies of America to be united under one head, whether it would be possible to keep in due order and government so wide and extended an empire, the difficulties of communication, of intercourse, of correspondence, and all other circumstances considered.

A voluntary association or coalition, at least a permanent one, is almost as difficult to be supposed: for fire and water are not more heterogeneous than the different colonies in North America. Nothing can exceed the jealousy and emulation which they possess in regard to each other. The inhabitants of Pennsylvania and New York have an inexhaustible source of animosity, in their jealousy for the trade of the Jerseys. Massachusetts Bay and Rhode Island, are not less interested in that of Connecticut. The West Indies are a common subject of emulation to them all. Even the limits and boundaries of each colony are a constant source of litigation. In short, such is the difference of character, of manners, of religion, of interest, of the different colonies, that I think, if I am not wholly ignorant of the human mind, were they left to themselves, there would soon be a civil war from one end of the continent to the other; while the Indians and negroes would, with better reason, impatiently watch the opportunity of exterminating them all together.

After all, however, supposing what I firmly believe will never take place, a permanent union or alliance of all the colonies, yet it could not be effectual, or productive of the event supposed; for such is the extent of coast settled by the American colonies that it can never be defended but by a maritime power: America must first be mistress of the sea before she can be independent, or mistress of herself. Suppose the colonies ever so populous; suppose them capable of maintaining 100,000 men constantly in arms, (a supposition in the highest degree extravagant), yet half a dozen frigates would with ease ravage and lay waste the whole country from end to end, without a possibility of their being able to prevent it; the country is so intersected by rivers, rivers of such magnitude as to render it impossible to build bridges over them, that all communication is in a manner cut off. An army under such circumstances could never act to any purpose or effect; its operations would be totally frustrated.

Further, a great part of the opulence and power of America depends upon her fisheries, and her commerce with the West Indies; she cannot subsist without them; but these would be entirely at the mercy of that power which might have the sovereignty of the seas. I conclude, therefore, that England, so long as she maintains her superiority in that respect, will also possess a superiority in America; but the moment she loses the empire of the one, she will be deprived of the sovereignty of the other: for were that empire to be held by France, Holland, or any other power, America, will, in all probability, be annexed to it. New establishments formed in the interior parts of America, will not come under this predicament; I should therefore think it the best policy to enlarge the present colonies, but not to establish fresh ones; for to suppose interior colonies to be of use to the mother country, by being a check upon those already settled, is to suppose what is contrary to experience, and the nature of things, viz. that men removed beyond the reach of power will be subordinate to it.

October 20, I embarked again on board the *Winchester*, for England; and arrived in Plymouth Sound the 21st of November, after a rough and tempestuous voyage.

Suggestions for Further Reading

Social Structure

Carl Bridenbaugh, *Myths and Realities, Societies of the Colonial South* (1963)*; Arthur M. Schlesinger, "The Aristocracy in Colonial America," *Proceedings of the Massachusetts Historical Society*, vol. 74 (1962), pp. 3–21; James Henretta, "Economic Development and Social Structure in Colonial Boston," *William and Mary Quarterly*, 3d series, vol. 22 (1965), pp. 75–92; Jackson T. Main, *Social Structure of Revolutionary America* (1965)*; Emory Evans, "The Rise and Decline of the Virginia Aristocracy in the Eighteenth Century," Darrett B. Rutman, ed., *The Old Dominion* (1965), pp. 62–78; Kenneth Lockridge, "Land, Population and the Evolution of New England Society, 1630–1790," *Past and Present*, no. 39 (April, 1968), pp. 62–80. Edmund Morgan, *The Puritan Family* (1966)*; Edmund Morgan, *Virginians at Home* (1952)*; John Demos, "Notes on Life in Plymouth Colony," *William and Mary Quarterly*, 2d series, vol. 22 (1965), pp. 264–286; "Families in Colonial Bristol, Rhode Island. An Exercise in Historical Demography," *William and Mary Quarterly*, 3d series, vol. 25 (1968), pp. 40–57; Philip J. Greven, Jr., "Family Structure in Seventeenth Century Andover, Massachusetts," *William and Mary Quarterly*, 3d series, vol. 23 (1966), pp. 234–256; Philip J. Greven, Jr. "Historical Demography and Colonial America: A Review Article," *William and Mary Quarterly*, 2d series, vol. 24 (1967), pp. 438–454; Frederick B. Tolles, *Meeting House and Counting House: The Quaker Merchants of Colonial Philadelphia* (1940).*

Religion and the Churches

Evarts B. Greene, *Religion and the State* (1959)*; Perry Miller, "The Contribution of the Protestant Churches to Religious Liberty in Colonial America," *Church History*, vol. 4 (1935), pp. 57–66; Sidney E. Mead, *The Lively Experiment* (1963)*; William W. Sweet, *Religion in Colonial America* (1942); H. Richard Niebuhr, *The Kingdom of God in America* (1959)*; *Religion in American Life*, J. W. Smith and A. L. Jamison, eds., vol. 1, (1961); *American Christianity*, H. Shelton Smith et al., eds., vol. 1, (1963); Allen Heimert, *Religion and the American Mind* (1966); Perry Miller, *Jonathan Edwards* (1967)*; Conrad Wright, *The Beginnings of Unitarianism* (1955)*; Edwin S. Gausted, *The Great Awakening in New England* (1957)*; Ola A. Winslow, *Jonathan Edwards* (1940)*.

Education

Bernard Bailyn, *Education in the Forming of American Society* (1960)*; Frederick Rudolph, *The American College and University* (1962)*; Beverly McAnear, "College Founding in the American Colonies, 1745–1776," *Mississippi Valley Historical Review*, vol. 42 (1955), pp. 24–44; Richard Hofstadter, *Academic Freedom in the Age of the College* (1955)*; Samuel E. Morison, *Three Centuries of Harvard* (1936); Edmund E. Morgan, *The Gentle Puritan: A Life of Ezra Stiles* (1962).

Colonial Culture

Max Savelle, *Seeds of Liberty* (1965)*; Louis B. Wright, *The Cultural Life of the American Colonies* (1957)*; Brooke Hindle, *The Pursuit of Science in Revolutionary America*, (1956)*; Oliver W. Larkin, *Art and Life in America* (1959); Richard M. Gummere, *The American Colonial Mind and the Classical Tradition* (1963); Frederick B. Tolles, "The Culture of Early Pennsylvania," *Pennsylvania Magazine of History and Biography*, vol. 81, (1957), pp. 119–137; John Clive and Bernard Bailyn, "England's Cultural Provinces, Scotland and America," *William and Mary Quarterly*, 3d series, vol. 14 (1957), pp. 200–213; Peter Gay, *A Loss of Mastery, Puritan Historians in Colonial America* (1966)*; Frederick B. Tolles, *James Logan and the Culture of Provincial America* (1957); Michael Kraus, *The Atlantic Civilization* (1949)*; Dirk J. Struik, *Yankee Science in the Making* (1948)*.

Chapter Six
The Colonial Legacy

In less than 200 years a new society took shape in British North America. On an undeveloped continent European colonists established the foundations of a great nation. They came to the New World hoping to improve their lot, not to transform institutions or to establish a new civilization. Even the Puritans, driven by a vision of establishing a Zion in the Wilderness, sought to re-establish an archaic Christian commonwealth they thought had once existed. Instead, Americans created something new, less by design than as the result of the inter-action of traditions and values, largely English, which they brought with them, and strange, unanticipated circumstances with which they were confronted in the New World.

Vast, open spaces, material abundance, and weak English control played havoc with the transit of familiar social patterns. By the middle of the eighteenth century, enlightened circles in Europe regarded America as a social laboratory of human happiness. Americans also came to believe that, once freed from religious superstition and oppressive institutions, man could use intelligence to reform society and improve his lot. The Abbe Raynal saw America "as the asylum of freedom, . . . the cradle of future nations, and the refuge of the distressed." "In America,"

wrote another admiring Frenchman, Hector St. John de Crèvecoeur, "every thing is modern, peaceful, and benign." Elsewhere
"misguided religious tyranny, and absurd laws, . . . depress and
afflict mankind." In the New World, however, laws were "simple
and just" and mankind had "regained the ancient dignity of our
species."

Americans also began to perceive themselves as "a new race
of men" well before they embarked on the road to revolution
and nationhood. They still considered themselves Englishmen
but they were also Americans. One became an American, not
simply by being born in the colonies, but by experiencing its
blessings. Whoever set foot in America and shared its bounty
became an American, regardless of previous national origin.
"*He* is an American," Crèvecoeur explained, "who, leaving behind him all his ancient prejudices and manners, receives new
ones from the new mode of life he has embraced, the new
government he obeys, and the new rank he holds." America
knows "properly speaking, no strangers; this is every person's
country."

The image of America taking shape in the colonies and
spreading through Europe was of a society which had liberated
man from the forces that enslaved people in the Old World.
The state was no longer man's master but his servant. Wealth
and power were no longer concentrated in the hands of a hereditary elite but was widely diffused. In the New World man experienced "a sort of resurrection," wrote Crèvecoeur. Previously
he had "simply vegetated; he now feels himself a man, because
he is treated as such . . . the laws of his own country had over-
looked him in his insignificancy; the laws of this country cover
him with their mantle."

Widespread distribution of land provided the dynamic force
behind this social transformation and principal form of wealth.
A freehold gave people dignity, independence, and the right to
vote. "He is become a freeholder, from perhaps a German boor—
he is now an American. . . . From nothing to start into being:
from a servant to the rank of a master; from being the slave

of some despotic prince to become a free man, invested with lands to which every municipal blessing is annexed." Crèvecoeur believed that a fundamental change occurred in personality. The American yeoman farmer forgot "that mechanism of subordination, that servility of disposition which poverty had taught him." The result was a liberation of human aspiration and energies.

Rising in the world once the accomplishment of a few, now became a possibility for many. "No sooner did Europeans breathe American air," Crèvecoeur insisted, "than he forms schemes, and embarks in designs he never would have thought of in his own country," because "human industry has acquired a boundless field to exert itself in." Opportunity unleashed ambition as men discovered that hard work, sobriety, and honesty brought rewards that no king, nobleman, or bishop could thwart or tax collector confiscate. A life of active enterprise bred among "the highest and the lowest a singular keenness of judgment, unassisted by any academic light." Common sense, based on practical experience, rather than "shining talents and university knowledge" was the source of truth. The farmer who perched his son atop the plough as he drove through his fields taught him the way to success: "I am now doing for him . . . what my father formerly did for me," said Crèvecoeur's American farmer. The child learned the simple lesson: "Here men are workers." Above all America offered salvation through work, salvation through individual enterprise. Through work people acquired property and with property they achieved worth: on "land is founded our rank, our freedom, our power as citizens, our importance as inhabitants." Yet Crèvecoeur sensed the danger of wealth as the measure of man's worth, as the means of liberation from the constraints of institutions.

Freedom of the Individual

Freedom was a two-edged sword. Corrupt institutions enslaved; weak or nonexistent ones could unleash the darkness as well as the light in man. America was not only a land of sober, decent farmers and merchants but of frontiersmen governed only by their passions, who preferred to drink and live by the gun than become industrious yeomen. Without the restraining influence of government or religion, man in the wilderness could descend into a state of war, each pitted against the other.

Crèvecoeur saw on the frontier the dark possibilities of the free individual. But he need not have looked to the outer edges of organized society for doubts. Ben Franklin, that living embodiment of the "new race of men," celebrated on two continents as the quintessential American—peaceful and benevolent, industrious and frugal, learned yet practical, democrat yet man of genius—found it possible to reconcile his conviction that man exists to do good with his belief that nothing must thwart Americans in their quest for wealth. Concerning the Indians, he once said, "If it be the design of Providence to extirpate these savages in order to make room for the cultivators of the earth, it seems not improbable that rum may be the appointed means. It has already annihilated all the tribes who formerly inhabited the sea coast."

Certain that God was on his side, the First American could sanction the destruction of one race for the "benefit" of another. The same incongruity touched Crèvecoeur when he visited Charleston, South Carolina. The richest colony in America, South Carolina was the home of the rice and indigo planters who cultivated large plantations with numerous slaves, dividing their time between their plantations and their mansions in Charleston, a city of wealth and luxury, "of joy, festivity, and happiness." No less than other Americans, colonial South Carolinians would some day revolt against Britain because they preferred to believe that "all men are created equal," "endowed by their Creator with certain unalienable rights," including "life, liberty, and the pursuit of happiness." Yet the basis of South Carolina society was slavery, an institution unknown in Britain itself. Crèvecoeur reported that in Charleston the "horrors of slavery are unseen" though they abound everywhere. People had become deaf to the cries of the suffering: "their hearts are hardened; they neither see, hear, nor feel for the woes of their poor slaves, from those whose painful labours all their wealth proceeds."

Herein lies the ambivalence of the colonial experience. Most Americans were in fact freer and materially better off than people anywhere else. The state was relatively weak and the individual enjoyed enormous scope within which to move, act, and think as he wished. The church also had lost much of its influence. Many lived remote from houses of worship, the state often failed to buttress the church, and growing confidence in human ability weakened dependence on the supernatural. Even the family lost some of the cohesive and stabilizing force it possessed in Europe. Children left home at an early age, set out on their own, as Ben Franklin did, often settling far from parents and relatives. They lived apart, among others like themselves, relying on their own exertions to sink or swim. The open spaces offered both escape and opportunity, escape from constraints that annoyed, opportunity to test one's powers against the environment.

Beginning in the 1760s Great Britain, required by its victory over the French in the Great War for Empire (1754–1761) to reorganize the empire, restricted American freedom. Threatened from without, the colonists perceived more clearly than before the extent to which their society had diverged from their English model. Forced to defend their way of life, the colonists identified the American cause with the cause of human freedom. They boasted, in the words of Crèvecoeur's farmer: "We have no princes, for whom we toil, starve, and bleed; we are the most perfect society now existing in the world. Here man is free as he ought to be." They went to war, they said, to remain that way.

When Crèvecoeur's countrymen read his glowing, idealized account of America, 500 abandoned their native land for the wilderness, settling in the Ohio Country where they died of famine and disease. Other newcomers, before and since, fared better. But none found in America an escape from history. Crèvecoeur himself recognized the paradox of America. Nowhere were men as well off yet even in the New World "one part of the human species are taught the art of shedding the blood of the other." The country where man was freest enslaved 20 percent of its population.

Throughout most of their history since becoming an independent nation, Americans have been torn between their vision of the free individual, and the gnawing realization that unrestrained individualism crushes the weak and debases the strong. Yet out of the colonial experience grew a vision of human liberty and equality that found expression in a revolution and a new nation. "Almost everywhere," Crèvecoeur concluded, "liberty, so natural to mankind, is refused, or rather enjoyed but by their tyrants; the word slave, is the appellation of every rank who adore as a divinity, a being worse then themselves."

INDEX

Adams, John, 121, 156
Africa, 8
Africans, in Spanish colonies, 12; *See* Slavery
Agriculture, 77–82: land systems, 77–78; tobacco production, 22, 70–81; rice, 79; wheat, 79, 81; exports, 78–79; indigo, 79; lumber, 79; plantations, origins and development, 80–81
Admiralty, 115
American national character, 1–2, 175–180
Andros, Edmund, 111
Arabs, 89
Azores, 8

Bacon, Nathaniel, 109
Bacon's Rebellion, 108–110
Baltimore family, 37–38, 106, 112
Baptists, 120, 153, 156
Berkeley, Gov. William, 108, 109
Bishop of London, 150
Board of Trade, 115
Boston, 32, 82, 146
Bradford, William, *Of Plymouth Plantation*, 42–66
Brown University, 156
Burnaby, Reverend Andrew, 160–172

Cabot, John and Sebastian, 16
Calvin, John, 29
Cambridge Agreement, 32
Canada, 11, 76
Carolinas, origins, 39, 80
Cathay Co., 16
Ceuta, 8
Charles I, 37, 114
Charles II, 40
Charleston, 82, 122
Chartered trading companies, 16–17
Churches, *See* Religion
Church of England, 14, 148, 149, 156
College of William & Mary, 155, 156
Colonial agents, 117
Colonial culture, 158–160: science, 158, 159; arts, 159
Colonial period, significance of, 3–4, 175–180
Columbia College, 157
Columbus, Christopher, 9, 10
Commerce: British merchants' role in, 81, 82–83; commercial centers, 81–83; imports and exports, 79–82; American merchants, 82–83; urbanization, 82–83; *See* Mercantilism
Congregationalists, 148–149

Connecticut, 36, 110, 111
Cortes, Hernando, 11
Cosby, Gov. William, 124
Crèvecouer, Hector St. John de, 4, 176–180
Cromwell, Oliver, 110
Cuba, 9, 13
Currency supply, 86–87

daGama, Vasco, 8
Delaware, 40
Dias, Bartolomew, 8
Dominion of New England, 110–113
Drake, Sir Francis, 7
Dutch, 39, 84, 110, 113, 159

East India Co., 21
East Indies, 9
Eastland Co., 16
Economic development, 67–89: standard of living, 67, 81, 87–88; labor recruitment, 23, 69–74; population growth, 69; immigration, 70–72; westward expansion, 74–76
Education: European antecedents, 154; in Massachusetts, 155; American needs, 154–157; colleges, 155–158
Edwards, Jonathan, 150, 152
Elizabeth I, 17, 30
England, Expansion, 13–18: Economic development, 14–17; conflict with Spain, 17; colonization methods, 20–21; Civil War (1641–1660), 21
English Civil War, 110
European Expansion, 6–18: Portugal, 7–9; Spain, 7, 11–13; psychological consequence, 10; varieties of colonization, 10–13; England, 7, 11, 13–18; France, 7, 11

Ferdinand and Isabella, 7
Fishing industry, 79
France, rivalry with Britain, 74–76
Franklin, Benjamin, 141–142, 157, 158, 159, 178, 179
Freedom of the press, 122, 124–138
Fundamental Orders of Connecticut, 36

Georgia, 40–42
Germans, 71, 121
Glorious Revolution, 111, 116
Government and Politics: Democratization, 103–105, 112–114, 122–124; European assumptions, 103–105; American developments 104–105; beginnings in America, 105–108; colonial governors, 107, 117–120; the Councils, 107, 116; local government, 107–108; political instability and rebellions, 108–113; British controls, 108–113, 114–118; colonial legislation, 106, 116–121; suffrage, 119; representation, 119; political parties, 120; factions, 120–121; interest groups, 120; elites, 120–121, 142–147; deference, 122–124
Great Awakening, 150–154
Great War for Empire (1754–61), 179

Half-way Covenant, 151
Hamilton, Andrew, 124
Harvard College, 155
Hat Act, 86
Headrights, 71, 77
Henry VIII, 13, 30
Hooker, Thomas, 36
House of Burgesses, 24, 106
Hudson River Valley, 78
Hutchinson, Anne, 35, 36, 147

Immigration, 70–72
Indians: Aztecs, 11; Incas, 11; Virginia, 24; European attitudes towards, 74–75
Indentured servants, 71–72
India, 8, 9
Intercolonial Wars, 76
Irish, 71
Iron Act, 86

James I, 22, 30, 31
James II, 39, 111
Jamestown, 21, 25, 109
Jefferson, Thomas, 157

Labor, 23, 69–74, 83
Land Systems, 77–78
Laud, William, 31
Leisler, Jacob, 112
Leisler's rebellion, 112

Levant Co., 16
London, 14, 15, 117
Long Island, 112
Louis XIV, 76
Luther, Martin, 14, 27

Maryland, 37–38, 77, 106
Mayflower, 31
Massachusetts, 101, 107, 110, 111, 155: Massachusetts Bay Co., 25–37, 33
Mayhew, Jonathan, 114
Mercantilism, 83–87, 115
Mexico, 11
Molasses Act, 85
Morris family, 124
Muscovy Co., 16

Navigation Acts, 84–85
New Jersey, 39, 123
North Africa, 9
North Carolina, 40, 108
New York, 39
New York City, 82, 147
Nicholson, Francis, 118

Oglethorpe, James E., 40

Parliament, 14, 31, 105, 114, 115, 117
Penn, William, 40
Pennsylvania, 40, 71, 121, 123, 149
Peru, 11
Philadelphia, 82, 141
Phillips, Thomas, 89
Pilgrims, 31, 42–66
Pizarro, Francisco, 11
Plantations, 80–81
Plymouth, Mass., 31
Pitt, William, 76
Population growth, 69–72
Portugal, overseas expansion, 7–9
Presbyterians, 156
Princeton, 156, 157
Proprietary colonies, 37–40
Privy Council, 114, 115
Prince Henry the Navigator, 8
Protestant Reformation, 13–14, 26–32, 147
Providence, R. I., 35, 82
Puritans, 26–37: Theology, 29–30; and Church of England, 30, 31, 34, 105; persecution in England, 31; social theory, 32–34; Con-gregationalism, 33–34; decline of Puritanism, 151–152

Quakers, 40, 121, 147, 149

Raleigh, Sir Walter, 21
Raynal, Abbé, 175
Religion: Freedom of, 40, 147–154; Church and state, 147–150; religion in Europe, 147; Denomina-tionalism, 150–154, 156; Revival-ism (Great Awakening) 150–154; secularism, 152–154; *See* Puritans, Protestant Reformation
Rhode Island, 35, 110, 111, 123, 149
Roanoke Island, 21
Roman Catholic Church, 149: Pro-testant Reformation, 13–14, 26, 28; Maryland 137, 148; Glorious Revolution, 111
Royal African Co., 89

Salem, 32, 34, 151
Salem witch trials, 151
Santo Domingo, 9
Scotch-Irish, 71, 121
Scots, 71
Secretary of State, 115
South Carolina, 39–40, 75, 121, 178
Spain: Overseas expansion, 7–13, 83; Spanish colonization system, 10–13; the Church, 11; rivalry with Britain, 75
Spanish Armada, 17
Shakespeare, William, 17
Slavery, 73–74, 178–179; *See Voyage of the Hannibal*, Plantations
Smith, Capt. John, 22, 23
Smyth, Sir Thomas, 21

Tobacco, 22, 78–79
Toleration Act, 38
Treasury, 115
Tudor dynasty, 13

Virginia, 73, 77, 107: Virginia Com-pany, 31, 106; origins, 21–22; failure, 22–25
Voyage of the Hannibal, 89–99

Walpole, Sir Robert, 116
Washington, George, 157
West Indies, 79, 82, 85, 89
Westward expansion, 74–76

Whitefield, George, 150
William of Orange, 112
Williams, Roger, 34, 35, 37, 147, 149
Winthrop, John, 32, 34, 35, 36, 106, 123

Winthrop Jr., John, 37
Woolen Act, 76

Yale, 155

Zenger, John Peter, 122, 124–138